"AND STILL,
I
CRY"

Duncan & Duncan, Inc., Publishers

AND STILL, I CRY

Duncan & Duncan, Inc., Publishers, Edgewood, MD 21040.

Telephone: (410) 538-5579   Fax (410) 538-5584

Library Of Congress Catalog Card Number: 90-086221
1. Biography   2. Abuse - physical, child, sexual
Barbara A. Robinson   3. Black women, in the South

ISBN 1-878647-01-6 PB

To protect the privacy of some of the innocent people involved in this true story, certain names and scenes may have been altered.

10 9 8 7 6 5

Dedication

To all of you who have so much faith in me, so much respect for me, and who place a high value on what I have to say, this book is dedicated to you. A simple *thank you* is too small to communicate my gratitude - but *thank you* for always being there for me. *Thank you* for allowing me to make my own mistakes, and make them I did, yet you never judged me.

Acknowledgments

This book is for a very beautiful young lady whom I love more than life itself, and who has been my greatest inspiration, my oldest daughter, Jericka. She has prodded me , encouraged me, scolded me, and begged me for years to write my biography so that it might be used to encourage other women never to give up their dreams. For you, little lady, my very special friend, and my precious first born, this book is for you.

I also thank my two surviving triplets, Jeanese and Jeanene. I have always called you twins because your sister, the third triplet, Jeanette, died seventeen days after she was born. You have both always made me so very proud of you.

To my very special last-born, my only son Jerome, Jr., whom I fondly call "Butchie", I don't know a mother alive who has bragged about her son more than I have bragged about you. Thank you for giving me so much joy and so much to brag about. You have filled my heart with pride and happiness.

And last but not least, to my beloved husband, Jerry, who has tolerated more from me than any wife could expect of a husband, thank you for always being there to support me through whatever I endeavored. You have been my strength and my motivating force in more ways than you could ever understand. You have been my lover, my husband, my buddy, my partner, my pal, and you're still my best friend. I know that the road has not been easy during the years we have spent together, but I am glad we stayed and grew together. I like who we have become.

The Story

Genesis

My father was dying of cancer and I flew back to a hospital in Tuskegee, Alabama to see him before he died. I wanted to ask him why he and my mother never married each other. I stood beside his bed and looked at the frail form who had been my tall, handsome father and who now weighed less than eighty pounds. There was a growth on the side of his neck about the size of a basketball. I felt pain and guilt that even today I cannot describe.

I wanted to ask him so many questions. I was feeling guilt because I had not taken the time to sit and talk with my father as an adult. The last time I had seen him was during a visit to Alabama when I was pregnant with the triplets and Jericka was only six months old. I wanted so much to tell him how much I loved him. I wanted so much to hear how he had spent his life, to ask him if he had missed me all those years, because I was his only child. I wanted so much for him to meet his grandchildren. I wanted so much to tell him how much I had cherished that doll he had given me for Christmas so many years ago. I regretted not knowing him in my adult life.

I had seen him on several nights after I learned that he was my father. Every Friday and Saturday night, all the "colored adult in-crowd" people gathered in the yard of the movie theater and the cafe. The ladies dressed in their fancy "sportin' clothes," as they were called, posing on the cars and flirting with the men. They went in and out of the theater and cafe, laughing. I knew that my father joined the crowd every weekend. I sat on Mama's front porch every weekend about the time the crowd started to gather and I waited to see him. I thought that he was the most handsome man I had ever seen.

Every time I saw him I ran to him and lifted my arms for him to pick me up. He was so tall, I barely came to his knees. He would lift me in his strong arms and hug me tightly. He always acknowledged my presence and said to his friends, "This is my daughter, my little girl. Don't she look just like her daddy? She got eyes just like me."

Then he gave me a quarter. A quarter was a lot of money to a little girl at that time. Although my mother never married my real father, I knew who he was. My grandmother's house was directly across the street from the only colored movie and the only colored cafe in Alexander City or Alex City, as we called it. I always wanted my mother to marry my real father, but she never did. Instead, she married a soldier named Frank Coffey, who lived in Columbus, Georgia and was stationed at Fort Benning, Georgia. She had met him one night while visiting her older sister, Maelizzie, who also lived in Columbus. I never did like Frank and during the years to come I grew to hate him or if it wasn't hate, the feeling of dislike was so intense it bordered on hate.

I was two years old when Mother married Frank. Immediately after she married him, my sister, Sandy, was born. Mother moved to Columbus to live with Frank and took Sandy with her. I remained in

Alex City living with Mama and Papa. Then, by contemporary societal standards, I was labeled an "illegitimate" child. What a heavy burden to put on anyone, much less a small child. Through no fault of the child's and particularly by society's standards and definition, illegitimacy carries a lot of negative consequences. Often the child does not have access to the father's surname; and if the biological father is married, his wife may not accept the child as part of her family.

I guess I am always talking about life in Alex City. That's because whenever I think about happiness, family love, family unity, the goodness of God, the beauty of the world, and "home folks" I think about "home," and "home" to me will always be Alex City.

Yet, I was always afraid of that house on 43 Laurel Street. I had seen my uncle and my grandfather die there, and somehow I always thought that they were haunting the house they loved so much. I remember when my Uncle Tom died in the room that we always called "Tom's room." I was afraid to go inside the house alone for months after he was buried.

Alex City was a small town, where the families knew each other and it seemed that everyone was related. I knew they were not all related, but there were so many kin folks living in Alex City that you got the feeling that we all were cousins. The old folks loved to tell ghost stories to the young folks. I always wondered how much was fiction and how much was fact. I never dismissed as nonsense that which I did not understand, such as the spirit world. Alex City was filled with very religious Baptists and Methodists. Almost all of the people who lived in our part of town were poor Blacks. Others who were even poorer than we lived in a section of the city called Lonesome.

Lonesome was just over the hill from where we lived, about a mile beyond my grandparents' house. The people who lived in Lonesome had to pass by my grandparents' house to get home. Lonesome was just as its name implies, lonesome. I never knew that it was a ghetto. In fact, I had never heard the word "ghetto," nor did I know the meaning of the word until I moved to Baltimore. I never knew that we were poor because everyone around us was in the same financial straits.

I just knew that Lonesome was a part of my hometown where the poorest colored people lived. All the roads in Lonesome were red dirt and all the houses were what we called "shotgun houses." One could stand on the front porch of a shotgun house and look straight through the house to the back yard. Some of the houses in Lonesome had been painted white when they were first built but had turned a dirty, dingy off-white from years of rain and cars splashing red mud on them. The houses had tin roofs and the paint had peeled off some from years of neglect. Others had not been painted at all. They were just shacks with their sides often supported by tree limbs. It's funny, but years later when I visited Africa, some of the African dwellings reminded me of the living conditions in Lonesome.

We, as a race of people, were not referred to as "Black" in those days. We were called "Colored." It was pronounced as if it were spelled "Cullud." Being called "Black" by whites was considered insulting because it was thought to be a reference to skin color rather than to a race of people or a way of life. We were called either "Negroes," "Nigras," or "Cullud."

Going to or coming from church, people had to pass by the only colored cemetery in Alex City, which was behind the town's largest colored Baptist church. The old folks often told stories of a dark shadow following them from the cemetery and turning into the yard of my grandparents' house as they passed by on their way home. My grandmother, who had ten children of her own, told the story of being alone in the house and hearing my grandfather call her name, although he had been dead for many years.

I remember her telling me that one night while she was in bed, the bed cover suddenly began to rise in the air as if someone were lifting it.

I asked, "Mama, weren't you afraid that the ghost would get you?"

She just laughed and replied, "That was probably Papa. He loved me and he loved you and our whole family. He wouldn't hurt me. He is probably coming back checking on us to make sure that we are all right." Sometimes I slept in Mama's bed with her and she told me stories until I fell asleep. How I loved that warm feeling I always got when I slept in Mama's bed! She always said, "Stop kicking and go to sleep or I'll make you get up and sleep in the chair all night by yourself." I just giggled and hugged her neck and kissed her on her cheeks. I knew she wouldn't make me get up.

You could always tell where the colored folks lived in those southern towns because in the white folks' sections, the streets were paved, there was bus service, and street lights. In the colored sections, the streets were unpaved, there was no bus service, and no street lights. However, in my hometown, God provided His own street lights. I have never seen nights as clear and the moon and stars as bright as they are in Alabama, except in Africa.

We lived on the corner of Laurel Street. Facing our house was old lady Ella Mosley's house. Ella was hard-of-hearing and she lived alone in an old, unpainted shack. Mama told me that Ella was related to our family somewhere down the line. Ella's house stood on a high hill and next to her lived Mrs. Lula Street. Mrs. Lula Street built a little shack onto her house and converted it into the only colored cafe in town after they tore down Sleepy Tucker's Cafe. Her cafe appropriately was called Lula Street's Cafe. Lula was not permitted to sell alcoholic beverages in the cafe because Alex City was "dry," which meant that alcoholic beverages had to be purchased outside the town at what were called ABC stores. However, bootleg corn liquor and home brew could be bought almost anywhere in Alex City.

My uncle Snook had been caught by the police for selling corn liquor so many times that they just stopped bothering him. In fact, the policemen became some of his best customers. Mrs. Lula Street's Cafe and the movie house across the street from Mama's, the Rex Theater, came years later. When I was about three or four years old, the only colored cafe in Alex City was called Sleepy Tucker's Cafe and Movie. The building that housed the cafe and movie was located right next to the white folks' graveyard.

Sleepy Tucker's Cafe was nothing more than a wooden building painted dingy yellow. On one side of the building was the cafe and on the other side was the movie house. The cafe consisted of a juke box, a potbellied stove for heat, wooden floors covered with sawdust, some booths around the sides of the walls leaving room for dancing, and the counter that served as a bar but displayed only soft drinks. However, home brew and corn liquor could be purchased for the asking.

The side that served as the movie house wasn't much better than the cafe. It was just a large room filled with rows of backless wooden benches and a large screen stood in the front of the room. We could go next door to the cafe to buy candy and other munchies such as potato chips and sodas, but there wasn't anything like the fresh popcorn that we have today.

The years we lived with my grandparents were days of fun and happiness for me. I think those were the only days I can remember being happy as a child. I called my grandmother, Mama, and my grandfather, Papa. Mama was more of a mother to me than my own mother.

Sometimes, however, I thought that my grandfather was the meanest man I ever knew. His method of disciplining us was to beat us with a very large switch. One day Sandy and I were fighting as we always did when Mother brought her to Alex City to stay with Mama and me. Papa said, "I'm tired of you two fighting and if I catch you fighting each other again, I will get three switches, one for each of you and one for me. I will make you two whip each other with the switches and if you don't whip each other, I'll whip both of you." Needless to say, we didn't fight with each other anymore when Papa was around because we knew how hard he could hit and we also knew that he was not kidding.

We didn't have inside plumbing in the house in Alex City. Our water came from a well out in the back yard. Papa drew the water from the well every day and it was always cool drinking water. To get to the toilet or the "outhouse," we had to travel a narrow trail that was covered with bushes and tall grass. A fence covered with vines and weeds ran the length of the trail from Mama's and Papa's house to the end of their property which was approximately three acres. The fence separated our property from our neighbor's.

We had to go through an orchard of fig trees, apple trees, plum trees, peach trees, and around behind the chicken house to get to the toilet. The trees, the trail, and the vines on the fence were infested with snakes. I was always so afraid to go to the toilet alone, because more than once I had seen snakes on the fence and crawling up the trees. Papa said they were just harmless garden snakes, but to me a snake was a snake.

Mama and Papa raised chickens and hogs on their property. Every Sunday Mama fried chicken and Papa made ice cream in the old, hand-cranked ice cream freezer that stayed on the back porch. To make strawberry ice cream, Papa poured Nehi strawberry sodas into the ice-cream mixture. The bucket had salt and dry ice packed around the outside of the container that held the ingredients for the ice cream. Mama called those ingredients "custard." She made the custard using eggs, vanilla, pure cream, and sugar. You can't find that kind of flavor today.

I often watched Papa or Mama go out into the chicken house, select a nice fat hen, hold it by the neck, wring it around and around a few times, then pull the chicken's head off. After the head had been pulled off, the headless carcass still jumped around on the ground for a few minutes. Mama would dip the chicken into boiling water and then pluck its feathers. She even cooked the chicken's feet.

I watched Papa select a fat pig from the pig pen, take an ax and hit the pig on the top of the head; the pig grunted and died. Mama made use of every part of the pig. We kids used the pig's bladder as a toy. We took a hollowed reed, stuck it into the top of the bladder and blew the bladder up like a balloon. Then we tied a string around the top of the bladder to keep the air from escaping and we played with the bladder like a ball.

I loved to go and spend the night with my great-grandmother. I called her Grandma. Grandma had a big white house that sat back from the road among huge trees. She lived on the other side of the city where the white folks lived. There was a fish pond in her front yard; fruit trees, and grapevines grew over a white picket fence. Grandma lived in a beautiful house built by my great-grandfather, who died before I was born. I thought Grandma was rich because her bathroom was on her porch and it flushed. I often accompanied Grandma when she went to clean the white folks' houses. Sometimes they gave Grandma biscuits they had saved from the previous day and Grandma carried them home for our supper.

To go to the store in the section where Grandma lived, it was necessary to walk through the white folks' neighborhood. The white folks' back yards connected to a trail that was used to get to the store, and Grandma's yard led to the trail.

One day while I was playing with some of the children who lived on the street behind Grandma's house, we heard a lot of crying and screaming coming from one of the white neighbor's houses. Being about four or five years old and naturally curious, we went to investigate. We learned that the screaming was coming from our nearest white neighbor's house. We ran over there and discovered that one of the little girls had been badly burned with an electric heater that was standing too close to the bathtub.

The heater had fallen on the little girl as she was getting out of the tub. I remember standing there in the white folks' bathroom looking at the red burned area on the little girl's body. At that moment, I became acutely aware of the difference in how her skin turned red when it was burned but mine did not when I was once scalded by boiling water. After a while, the girl's parents came into the room to make the little "colored children" leave.

Because I had been in the house of the white folks, my childish mind told me that we were friendly with each other. Therefore, I always made it a point to go over and speak whenever I saw one of the white neighbors in the back yard. When they didn't respond, I told myself they must not have heard me. I believed that because I had not been taught racism and prejudice.

Once when I was walking through the trail to go to the store, the little white girl's father was in the back yard chopping wood. I said, "Hello," but he did not speak. He didn't even raise his head to acknowledge that I was standing there. Being a child and trusting everyone as children often do, I thought that he didn't hear me. Wanting to prove that I was friendly and that I liked him, I again said, "Hello," and again he ignored me. I went closer and spoke again and again, but he still ignored me and just kept chopping wood.

I reasoned that the noise from chopping the wood had drowned out my voice. So when he slowly started to look up at me, I was standing there smiling, making a waving gesture with my hand, preparing to speak again, but the look on his face stopped me cold. I had never seen a look like that before. I was so scared that I turned around and ran as fast as I could back to Grandma's house. I forgot that I was on my way to the store. I thought that surely he was going to chop me with that ax he was holding. I had just been introduced to racism and the look I didn't recognize was called "hate." Grandma told me that but I could not understand what "hate" meant.

Although Mother eventually made me move to Columbus, Georgia to live with her and Frank, I always went back to Alex City every summer as soon as the school year was over. Sometimes I didn't even wait to get my report card before I left Columbus. I was eager to go "home." I never thought of Columbus as home.

Georgia, My Hell

When Mother took me to live in Columbus, I was approximately four or five years old and in the second grade. I cried because it was as if I were being taken from my home to a strange land into a stranger's house who didn't want me there. That was, in fact, exactly what was happening to me. I imagine that was the way the slaves felt hundreds of years ago when they were taken from their native African home, from family members who loved them, and into a hostile land filled with strangers who neither wanted them nor respected them.

Fort Benning, Georgia, where Frank was stationed, was only about nine miles from Columbus. Frank's grandfather's name was William Coffey, but everyone called him Will. Frank's grandmother's name was Lucinda Coffey, but everyone called her Cindy. We called Mr. Coffey, Big Papa, and we called Mrs. Coffey, Big Mama. Big Papa treated me all right, but Big Mama disliked me and was constantly doing mean things to hurt me when Mother was not around. She didn't like me because I was not Frank's biological daughter.

When Mother and Frank went out at night, Big Mama locked me out of the house, gave Sandy ice cream and candy, and wouldn't give me any. She would talk in a loud voice to Sandy so that I could hear her through the locked door. She would say, "Ummmmmmmmm, ain't dis ice cream good, Baby? We won't gib dat old gal none. She ain't none yo suster noway. She ain't got no daddy lack you." I could hear Sandy laughing at me. I know now that she was too young to understand what was happening at the time, but it sure hurt. Big Mama called me names such as "Bastard" and "Illegitimate." I didn't know what those words meant, but from the way she was saying them, I knew they must have been bad.

When Mother came home, I told her how Big Mama had treated me. Mother tried to comfort me and told me, "That's all right, Baby. You didn't want that old ice cream anyway. I'll buy you some tomorrow when the ice cream man comes by." But it wasn't the candy or the ice cream that I wanted - I just wanted Big Mama to like me. I just wanted to feel like a part of the family. I wanted her to treat me like she did Sandy, but she never did.

I didn't like living with Big Mama and Big Papa. Mother, Sandy, Frank (he forced me to call him Daddy), and I lived in one small room off the backporch of Big Mama's house. Sandy and I slept in one small bed and Mother and Frank slept in a double bed. I was afraid to stay in that room alone when Frank and Mother went out at night. Not only did Big Mama lock me out of the house, she also would scare me by saying that she was going to get Obie and he was going to take me to the river in a sack and drown me.

Obie was a blind man who lived up the street from Big Mama's. He was a big, robust man, and very dark. He always wore ragged and dirty clothes, and talked in a very loud voice. Obie was always talking about beating somebody up. There were stories that Obie had beaten a man to death. People said that Obie talked nice to the man until he got close enough to grab him. When the man was within Obie's reach,

Obie held the man with one hand and beat him with the other. He didn't get any time in jail because he was blind and the plea was self-defense. I don't know how true that story was but it sure frightened the neighbors.

One day Big Mama said to me, "One of dese heah nights when yo mama goes out wid Junior (that's what they called Frank), I'm gonna lock you in de closet and den I'm gonna git Obie and he gonna take yo way from heah and kill you. And when yo mama gits home and finds you gone, she ain't gonna care cause she be glad yo gone cause you jist a pest anyhow, and you only in de way of dem being happy." Big Mama also said that if I cried when she locked me out and if I told Mother what she said to me, she was going to get Obie the very next day because he didn't like little girls who cried. I believed everything she said.

One night Big Mama stood in the front door and called out my name in a deep voice and pretended that she was Obie coming after me. I ran and hid under our bed and stayed there until Mother and Frank returned home. From that night on, I always hid under the bed whenever Mother went out. For a long time Mother could not understand why she always came home and found me asleep either under the bed, in a corner, or in the clothes closet hiding in the dark.

Only after we moved from Big Mama's house and I grew older did I realize that Big Mama had made up those lies. Yet, she went to church every Sunday, sat in the front row, and shouted louder than anyone.

Big Papa was a small-built man and we called him "hen-pecked." Big Mama was always cursing at him and he just said, "Aw, Cindy," and went on his way. He knew how she was treating me, but he wouldn't say anything about it to her or to Mother and Frank. He seemed to be afraid of her. When she locked me out, he just sat on the front porch and didn't interfere. However, Big Mama had a sister we called, Aunt Miss. One day Aunt Miss said to Mother, "Louise, you take your children away from here. Don't let Cindy break up your home and don't let her make a difference between your children."

Big Mama and Big Papa owned two dogs they kept tied in the back yard, one named Blackie and the other called Bob. Bob was a mean old dog. He wouldn't let anyone get close to him or feed him, except Big Mama. She treated those dogs as mean as she treated me. The dogs were always dirty and had a terrible odor.

Although there was only one kitchen and one refrigerator at Big Mama's house, Mother kept our food separate from Big Mama's. Mother also cooked separately for our family. Mother said she didn't want any trouble from Big Mama about the food. One day Mother had prepared dinner for us and Sandy and I were sitting at the kitchen table, eating. The kitchen was just off the back porch. It was necessary to walk out of the main part of the house and pass the room where we stayed to get to the kitchen. I never did like cats and Big Mama had an old cat that always rubbed against my legs every chance she got. The cat acted as if she knew that I didn't like her and I always thought that she rubbed against me just to antagonize me.

The cat was rubbing against my leg as I sat at the kitchen table on that particular day, but I didn't say anything because I didn't want to cause any trouble between Mother and Big Mama. Big Mama always rolled her eyes at me when Mother was not looking; therefore, I just sat there and did not move. I asked Mother for another piece of bread and Big Mama said to me in a hateful tone of voice, "You ain't gonna eat up all dem vittles from Junior. You're jist lak dat ol dog out dare in de back yard, always begging fur food."

When Big Mama said that, she was walking out of the kitchen giving me mean looks over her shoulder. Mother hurried and put the food she was holding on the table and caught Big Mama just as she walked onto the back porch. Mother hit Big Mama so hard she knocked her down. Before Big Mama had a chance to get up, Mother grabbed the broom and jumped on top of her. Mother straddled Big

Mama as if she were riding a horse. Mother put the broom handle across Big Mama's neck and began choking her with the broom handle.

Big Mama was lying on the floor kicking and screaming so loudly that the neighbors came to their windows to see what all the noise was about. Mrs. Whitaker, the old lady whose back yard joined Big Mama's, came running to try to pull Mother off Big Mama. But Mother was too angry. She held the broom handle across Big Mama's throat with her knees while she kept punching Big Mama with her fists.

She was still beating on Big Mama with her fists when two men who were walking by came to see what the screaming was all about. By that time, a crowd had gathered in Big Mama's yard. It took both of the men to pull Mother off Big Mama. Mother was still trying to kick Big Mama as they were pulling her off. I was so scared, I thought Mother was going to kill Big Mama for sure. Come to think of it, as angry as Mother was that day, she probably would have killed her if those men hadn't stopped the fight.

I had never seen Mother that angry. Mother just kept crying and screaming at Big Mama, saying over and over, "I'm tired of you mistreating my child. I'll kill you. I'll kill you, you hateful old witch."

Mother grabbed me and Sandy and walked around the corner to Maelizzie's and Bob's house. The entire time we were walking to Maelizzie's house, Mother was crying and saying over and over, "I'll never sleep in that house again as long as I live," and she made good on her promise.

Frank was on the base all day and came home at night. When he came home that night and found that we had left Big Mama's house and had gone to Maelizzie's, he came around for us. Mother told him what had happened. She also told him that she would not stay with Big Mama anymore because she would end up killing that "evil old woman about my child." Big Mama didn't want Frank to marry Mother in the first place.

"Marryin dat woman wid all dem chillun," she had said, although I was the only child Mother had at that time.

We stayed with Maelizzie and Bob for a while. Again, all four of us slept in the same room, but that time Sandy and I slept on the sofa. We stayed there until Frank bought a house in East Wynnton, a section of Columbus where colored folks could buy cheap houses. Mother had refused to move again until Frank bought us a house of our own. She said she was tired of living with someone else and being cramped in one small room.

We moved into a shotgun house on a street where every house on one side of the street stood in a row and looked exactly alike. Each one was painted white and you could stand on the front porch and look into the back yard by looking directly through the front door (just like the houses in Lonesome except those were not dirty white). That was what we called "home" and that was where my hell continued.

Mable, Frank's only sister, often came to visit us when we first moved to East Wynnton. Each time she came, she brought a gift for Sandy and nothing for me, promising to bring me something "next time." It was always the same story, but she never kept her promise. Once she came to visit and bought Sandy two pieces of material from which two outfits were to be made for Sandy. Mother must have seen the hurt in my face because she gave the cloth back to Mable and said, "Keep this until you can afford presents for both of my children. And if you cannot afford two, please don't bring any." Mable took the cloth and left and never visited us again.

I was six years old when Mother enrolled us in Brookfield Elementary School after we moved to East Wynnton. Brookfield was a two-room schoolhouse that stood upon a hill in a colored residential community and was surrounded by old houses and dirt roads. Brookfield had two teachers, Miss Fair and Miss Sanford. Miss Sanford was also the principal.

There were four grades at Brookfield, the first, second, third, and fourth grades. In each room, one teacher taught two grades every day. In one room, Miss Fair taught the first and second grades while Miss Sanford taught the third and fourth grades in the other room. Students in the same grades sat together on one side of the room. For example, in Miss Fair's room the first graders sat on the left side of the room and the second graders sat on the right side.

That held true for Miss Sanford's classes; the third grade students sat on one side of the room and the fourth grade students sat on the opposite side. Each teacher moved back and forth effortlessly teaching different subjects to different grades of students. Miss Fair and Miss Sanford didn't seem to have any trouble keeping lessons straight. There was even enough time for the teachers to give us individual attention. We had to do our homework before we left school, so the teachers could assist us if needed.

The teachers also often invited us to their homes and entertained us by playing games, and they treated us with cookies, ice cream, cake, and other goodies. The first time I ever won anything in my life was when I won a checkerboard game as a prize for playing bingo at Miss Sanford's house.

It was at Brookfield Elementary School that Janie Mary and I met when we both were in the second grade. We have remained friends for life. Janie and I were inseparable all during high school. We were in the same classes throughout school until we left for college, each going to a different college. I went where I could afford to go and Janie went where she had relatives.

Brookfield was an old school. It didn't have inside plumbing, the toilets were outside on the playground, and twice a week a truck came and took the waste containers out of the little wooden shacks that served as our toilets and replaced them with clean containers. We could smell the truck as soon as it came into the neighborhood. We kids called the truck, the "do-do truck."

Brookfield was heated by potbellied stoves that stood in the front of each classroom. The janitor was responsible for making sure that the school was warm before classes began. We hung our coats at the back of the room. There were not any cloakrooms, just nails driven into the walls from which we hung our coats and sweaters.

Miss Sanford and Miss Fair meant business. When they told us to do something, we did it. There was no question about what our parents would say or do if we got a whipping from our teacher. If I went home and told my mother that the teacher had whipped me, I received another whipping at home for misbehaving in school; "acting up in school" was what my mother called it.

Miss Sanford's and Miss Fair's disciplining method was to hit us kids across the palm of the hand with a strap made by cutting a belt or a razor strop into halves and nailing them to a piece of wood that served as a handle.

A razor strop is a very thick leather strap used to sharpen straight razors. Frank used them all the time. He would double them and use them to beat us until we were blistered or he would use ironing cords, not the thin ones of today, but the thick electric cords with elastic binding.

If a child went to school without bathing and one of the teachers smelled him or her, that child was sent back home to bathe and then return to school. We could not wear dirty clothes to school in Miss Sanford's and Miss Fair's classes. They said the same thing that my mother always said, "If you don't have but one dress or one pair of pants, keep them clean. They may be torn but they can at least be clean."

Bobby King was my first boyfriend. Mother gave me a birthday party for my sixth birthday and Bobby King came to my party. I really liked him. He was thin, fair-complexioned, and very good looking. He brought me a birthday present in a small box all wrapped in birthday paper. When he gave it to me, he made a bow like people do when being introduced to royalty. He lowered his head, stretched out his hand with the present and said in a exaggerated slow southern drawl, "Hit's mighty little, but hit costs mighty heap." I opened the box and discovered a ring. I thought the ring meant that he and I were engaged, but it soon turned green on my finger and made it swell so Mother made me throw it away. Later I learned that Bobby had found the ring in a box of *Cracker Jacks*. (At that time, *Cracker Jacks* were five cents a box.)

I was about seven years old when I was first introduced to real terror. I came home from school one day when I was in either the third or fourth grade and Frank was at home alone. Mother was at work. Our house didn't have a living room. There were two bedrooms, a kitchen, and the toilet was on the backporch. Frank and Mother shared the front room as their bedroom and Sandy and I shared the second room as our bedroom.

Mother's and Frank's room was heated by a fireplace. My and Sandy's room was heated by a potbellied stove. Each night Sandy and I had to bring in the coal and kindling that would be used to make the fire the next morning. We each did the chores on alternate nights. By the time my brother was born, another bedroom had been added to the house. Mother had forced Frank to add the extra room because she kept insisting that Sandy and I needed a place to entertain our friends.

Frank didn't want to provide a place for me to receive company. I couldn't have any boyfriends and he wanted to have me all to himself. He wrote all of that to me in love letters I often found in my school books next to my homework.

As I said, Frank was at home alone on this particular day. I came home from school and saw his green 98 Oldsmobile parked outside in front of the house. I walked into the house through the back door and entered through our bedroom. "Hello, Daddy, I'm home," I called as I entered the house and put down my school books.

"Hi Baby," Frank responded. "Come here and give Daddy a kiss," he said, stretching out his arms to me. I walked into the room and Frank was lying on the bed fondling his penis. I later learned that he was masturbating but I didn't know that at the time. I just knew that he was doing something I should not see and did not want to see.

I walked farther into the room and said, "Hi, Daddy."

Again Frank spoke and said, "Come over here and give Daddy a kiss. You ain't scared of Daddy, is you?"

"No sir," I responded, afraid to go near him, yet afraid not to. I was very young, but I knew that what he was doing was bad. That was the first time I had ever seen a man's penis and I was terrified. But I was afraid not to go over and kiss him because he could be awfully mean when he was crossed. He not only beat us kids, he also took his anger out on Mother. I knew how violent he could get and because I was at home alone with him, I knew that I had better obey him or risk being beaten.

I reluctantly walked over to the bed and kissed him. He pulled me down on top of him, kissed me, and put his tongue into my mouth. I had heard kids talk about "French Kissing" where a boy sticks his tongue in the girl's mouth when he is kissing her, but I didn't think that fathers were supposed to do that to their daughters. Frank began to move his body the way I had heard the boys and girls talk about at school. He started kissing me more and moving faster and making sounds in his throat. I felt his penis get harder and I got really scared. He tried to pull my dress up and I kept pulling it down. He tried to spread my legs open and I jumped down and ran and hid in the clothes closet behind the bag of dirty clothes.

Frank kept calling me and said, "If you don't come out and see what Daddy wants, you is going to git a beatin'." I would not come out of that closet. I stayed in there until Mother came home from work.

From that day on, if I was the first to come home from school, I looked to see if Frank's car was parked in front of the house. If it was, I slipped into the house through my bedroom window and hid in the closet until Mother came home. I hated that closet. It was dark and musty, and dirty laundry was stored there until Mother could wash. She only washed on Mondays, so there were always lots of dirty clothes in the closet, plus winter clothes and anything else not regularly used.

Moreover, there were mice, roaches, and spiders in the closet. Many days I sat in that closet and felt mice run across my feet, spider webs on my face and on my arms, and spiders and roaches crawling over my body, but I was too scared to scream. I was more afraid of Frank than I was of what was in the closet.

The closet soon became my refuge and my only protection. I used that closet not only to hide from Frank but to hide from Mother when she had been drinking and wanted to beat me. It always seemed that although she protected me from Big Mama, it was me she would single out to beat when she was drinking. When she was drunk, she also accused me of being interested in Frank. Now, as I think back over the years, she was acting as though I was another woman trying to take her husband from her, as though I was her competition.

One night I awoke and Frank was bending over me as I lay in bed beside Sandy. Sandy was asleep and didn't hear Frank as he crept into our bedroom. When I awoke, Frank had one hand under the bed cover fondling my breast and was masturbating with his other hand.

I said to him, "If you don't leave me alone, I am going to tell my mother on you." He ran back into his bedroom. The following morning I told mother I had something to tell her when I came home from school. She was in a hurry to go to work at the cleaners and I wanted time to talk to her about Frank.

When I came home from school that afternoon, Mother was already at home and had been drinking. She must have left work early and stopped to get a drink as she often did. Because I couldn't talk to her when she was like that, I went to Janie's house as I usually did.

That day, Frank came home with some of his army buddies. His buddies were teasing me about being pretty and said I was going to break some man's heart someday. The more they talked about how some man was going to be glad to get a pretty wife like I was going to become some day, the angrier Frank became. After his friends left, Frank tried to grab me and kiss me. I pulled away from him and ran. He said, "Aw nigga, you know you pretty, but ain't nobody gonna touch you but me and if you say anything, I'll beat you and your druken mother."

The next day when Mother was sober, I said, "Mother, make Daddy leave me alone. He is always bothering me when you are not around. He even bothers me when I am asleep."

She asked, "What do you mean, bothering you?"

I felt uncomfortable; it wasn't that she was asking me questions; it was the way she was asking, in an accusing tone of voice. I said, "You know, playing with my breast and my private" (meaning my vagina). Mother slapped me and said that she did not want to hear that filthy talk anymore. I went away and sat by myself and cried. I felt alone in the world and I began to wonder what I had done to make Frank act like that towards me. I was eight years old at the time.

Once Frank was preparing to drive somewhere. I don't remember where he was going but he told me to come and go with him. I knew he would try to feel all over my body as he usually did when we were alone in the car; therefore, I didn't want to go. He always tried to put his hand under my dress and kept feeling my breast. I always ran and hid when I saw him putting on his clothes to go somewhere so that he would not tell me to go with him.

This time I looked at my mother who was sitting next to the pot-bellied stove in Sandy's and my bedroom. I was hoping she would intervene and tell me I couldn't go. I had told her what Frank was doing to me and I was pleading with my eyes for her to tell me that I could not go with him. But she didn't interpret the message as one asking, indeed begging, for her help. Instead, she took off her shoe, threw it at me, and hit me in my back so hard that it knocked the wind out of me.

Mother yelled, "You don't be turning around looking at me like some woman going out the door with my husband." When the shoe hit me, it hurt, but it did not hurt as badly as I pretended. I began to cry as loud and as hard as I could and ran outside. That was the way I got out of going with Frank that day.

Soon after that Frank was transferred to Fort Dix, New Jersey. Mother, Sandy and I followed as soon as he found a place for us to live. Before we went to New Jersey, we stayed in New York with my Aunt Cara for two months. My Aunts Sadie and Ophelia also lived in New York. My Aunt Willie and Uncle W.L. moved to New York some years later. Just as Sadie was murdered in New York, W.L. was also found dead. His body was found lying in an alley, frozen. His coat, shoes, and socks were missing. His death was ruled "suspicious."

Sadie spent a lot of time with Sandy and me. She took us to Central Park, Radio City Music Hall, and to the movies. It was not unusual for us to go to two or three movies in one day. Musicals were very popular in the 1940s and 1950s and we all loved musicals. Sadie was just like a big kid, with her pretty self, going to all those movies in one day. Eating frankfurters we got from street vendors was just as much fun for Sadie as it was for Sandy and me. Sadie was always taking us somewhere. I often thought that she loved me more than my mother did. Foolish thoughts for a love-starved little girl.

Unfortunately, our visit to New York was during the polio epidemic. A cure for the deadly disease had not yet been discovered and people had begun to panic and were worried about being in large crowds. Places where large crowds were common, such as Central Park, suddenly became almost deserted. Therefore, Sadie did not take us to all the places she had planned for fear of us contacting the disease.

Living in a New York apartment and being exposed to cultures of various people was absolutely fascinating to Sandy and me. We were just southern country girls who had never been "up North" before.

When summer ended, Frank found us a room in a house in Trenton, New Jersey where other military families lived. Sandy and I slept in one small twin bed and Mother and Frank slept in a large double bed in the same room. Mother enrolled us in Parker Elementary School. Frank commuted each day to and from the army base at Fort Dix.

Mother found a job in a cleaners about two blocks from the house, and every weekend she resumed drinking. Frank always bought her alcohol and when she was drunk they would fight and he would leave. I always said that he wanted her to get drunk so that he would have an excuse to stay away from home or to leave the house. All the kids in the neighborhood teased us about how they often saw Frank with other women. I knew that he was having an affair with one of the women who lived in our rooming house.

The woman's little girl told me one day, "Your daddy took my mama to the movies and then he spent the night with us." I didn't mention it to Mother because it would just cause a fight, but she found out about it anyway. When she did, we moved across the street with a private family named Williams. Still, all four of us lived in one room.

Sandy and I were not allowed to go outside when our parents were not at home, which meant that we stayed in the small room when we came home from school. Mother never came home until it was dark and Frank would beat us if we were outside after sunset. We ran home many times trying to beat the sun.

We were constantly teased by the other children because we couldn't go outside and play, which left us out of the crowd. They called us "jail birds" and said that we were in prison. Sometimes I felt as if we were in prison because we had such limited freedom. Weeks often passed during which we were forced to remain in our tiny room looking out the window at the neighborhood children playing. Because we were not permitted to go outside and play with them, we were often victims of planned fights. I told my mother, but she didn't believe me. She just assumed that I was lying to get outside to play.

Planned fights worked like this. A kid would say to Sandy and me, "I heard you been talking about me behind my back. I'm going to beat you up after school," or " somebody told me you been talking about my mama. I'm going to wait for you after school and beat your ass." Of course none of that was true. We had not said any of those things, but the gang encouraged this behavior and, sure enough, the kids would be waiting after school to fight us.

The Williams family had three children, an older daughter, Emily, who was about my age (10 or 11) and stuttered very badly; a son called, Jimbo, who was about Sandy's age (7 or 8); and a younger daughter, Kathy, who was about five years old. They all teased Sandy and me, because we were not allowed to go outside, and they called us names because our mother drank and our parents fought all the time.

My memories of Trenton are painful ones. I cannot remember being happy or enjoying myself during the entire year we lived there. We were constantly fighting, because of the way that kids teased us about our parents. The neighborhood kids would stand outside our windows and listen to Frank beat Sandy, me, and Mother. We never did anything to deserve the type of beatings he gave us. He didn't beat Sandy as often as he beat me. It seemed that Mother was extra hard on me in order to prove to Frank that she was on his side, because I was not his daughter. Years later I came to realize that was not true, but that was the way I felt at the time.

After a year in Trenton, Frank was transferred back to Fort Benning, Georgia. When we were preparing to leave Trenton, the kids on our block had us so afraid of them that we believed them when they said, "Don't go back down South and talk about us. We will find out if you do `cause we got connections and if we find out that you did say something about us behind our backs, we will come down to Georgia and beat you up." And we believed them. That's how low our self-esteem was.

When we moved back to Columbus, things got worse for me. I managed to stay out of Frank's way as much as I could. All I wanted was to have some place to stay until I finished high school so that I could go to college. That was my dream for as long as I could remember. I never thought of not having enough money to go to college. I just knew that when the time came, the money would come from somewhere. Hoping that I could win a scholarship was the main reason I tried so hard to remain on the honor roll. I had always wanted to major in journalism because I loved to write.

However, one of my teachers told me there wasn't any money to be made in journalism and that I should become either a doctor or a lawyer. I decided on medicine, although I could not stand the sight of blood. Later I realized it was a mistake to abandon my dream of becoming a writer because someone discouraged me. I was allowing someone else to define my limitations.

When we returned to Columbus, Mother enrolled us in Radcliff Elementary School. I was in the sixth grade. I remained an "A" student throughout the entire time I was in school. I was also a leader in all activities I undertook, including being the editor of the school paper.

I wrote a column called, *The Editor Speaks*. I wrote another column called, *Smile Awhile*, which featured jokes that I collected. When the school library held contests to see which student could read the most books within a month, I always won first prize.

When I was in the ninth grade, while leafing through my notebook in school looking for the previous night's homework, I found a letter Frank had written to me on one of the pages in the notebook.

In it he said how much he loved me and how he wanted to make love to me by doing things to me that I should not let anybody else but him do. I destroyed the letter and went into the toilet and cried. Janie came into the toilet behind me and I told her about the letter. She confessed that Frank was the reason she had stopped visiting me as often as she once did. She had stopped by our house and asked Frank if I was at home and he lied and told her that I was in the house. When she went into the house looking for me, he followed her and tried to force her onto the bed. She pushed him away and ran home.

I stayed out of his way as much as I could. I always found reasons to stay late after school so that Mother would get home before me. I joined every organization I could. I volunteered to wash the erasers and blackboards after school. Sometimes I think one of the reasons I did so well in school was because I spent so much time in the library after school, afraid to go home.

When I was in the ninth grade, Frank started dating my class-mates and continued to do so until we graduated from high school. Almost every weekend some of my classmates came and told me what a good time they had with my father.

Frank was not a good-looking man, although he thought he looked great! He was dark-complexioned, weighed over three hun-dred pounds, stood about six feet tall, and had big bulging eyes. He didn't have a bad grade of hair and he kept it slicked down and combed back from his face. I often watched him stand in front of the mirror for long periods of time admiring himself. He reminded me of a bullfrog with his big eyes and funny-shaped head.

I remember once when we were living with Big Mama, Frank overheard Sandy say that she wished he gad gotten killed when he was overseas. He beat her for saying that, but I always felt that he should have been filled with grief that his own child disliked him enough to wish that he was dead. Beating her only made her dislike him more. He seemed to think that violence would solve everything, but it solved nothing.

One night Frank and Mother were in the backyard fighting. When Frank and Mother fought, it wasn't just him slapping her around. They fought to try to hurt each other. They fought with knives, guns, ice picks, razors, boiling water, hot grease, baseball bats, and anything else that they could use to really hurt each other. Mother was no match for him because she was always drunk when they fought. Yet, she would not give up. When he knocked her down, she got right back up and went after him again. She was like a wild woman. He never hit her when she was sober. He cursed her and called her vile names, but he would not hit her. Sandy and I always said he was afraid of Mother when she could defend herself. To me he was a coward and a bully. He used his size to intimidate people.

Our neighbors had long stopped caring or calling the police when they heard Frank and Mother fighting. On this particular night, Frank was beating Mother with his fists. I came to hate him the way I did because he was too big and strong to take his frustrations out on his family, but he did it anyway. Sandy was pretending to be asleep, as she often did when they were fighting.

I could never sleep when they were fighting. I was always trying to protect Mother. Frank knocked Mother down and began kicking her. She was yelling, "I know you want to kill me so you can have Barbran. She told me what you been trying to do to her. I know all about it."

When Mother said that Frank flew into a rage. He grabbed me by my hair and jerked me to the ground. He picked up the broom that was laying in the backyard and hit me so hard across my back with the handle that it broke off. Then he knocked me down and continued to beat me. While he was beating me, he was cursing and yelling, "That no good druken bitch you call your mother ain't shit and neither is you." Then he kicked me as I lay on the ground.

About four houses up the street from our house was what we called, the tar-road. It was a paved road where some well-to-do black families lived and it was the beginning of the white folks' section. The streets in our neighborhood were all dirt roads, just like in Alabama. Mother had run up the street to the tar-road while Frank was beating me. When he realized she had run off, he ran after her with the broken broom handle and I ran behind him. I didn't know what I was going to do, I just knew that I had to protect my mother from that crazy man.

When he caught Mother, he hit her with his fists and knocked her down and began beating her with the broom handle. I pleaded with him not to hit her anymore. He turned around to face me with the most horrible expression that I had ever seen. He swung the broom handle and hit me. The blow knocked me down and knocked the breath out of me.

At that moment I thought that he was going to kill me and Mother. He turned back to Mother and began kicking her and beating her. He said to me, "I'm gonna beat your mammie until you tell her that you wuz lying when you said dat shit about me." I begged and pleaded with him to stop but he just kept hitting her harder and harder.

Finally, I said that I had lied. Secretly I think that Mother wanted to believe I had lied. After I said that I had lied, he stopped beating Mother. He just walked back to his car and drove away. I crawled over to where Mother was lying and helped her home.

It seemed that every time Mother was drunk, which began as almost every weekend and then every other day, she would find an excuse to beat me and accuse me of having an affair with Frank. I don't know why Sandy never woke when Frank was bothering me at night. We slept together in the same bed, but she never woke up and when I told her about it the next day, she would not believe me.

One night Mother had been drinking and she was accusing me of going with Frank. She was calling me a bitch, a whore; saying that I was no good. She always called Frank by his last name. She said, "Coffey was right, you ain't no damn good. You are leading Sandy to follow in your footsteps. You try to pretend to be so innocent, `Miss Goody Two Shoes.' You're a bad influence on Sandy." The truth was that Sandy was having sex with boys and I was still a virgin. I spent all my time reading or writing. Sandy spent her time other ways, yet Mother and Frank always blamed me.

That night she kept telling me how bad I was and I kept denying it; that made her furious. She flew into a rage, picked up a shovel that was used to take ashes out of the stove, and tried to hit me on the head with it. I put my hand up to prevent the blow and the shovel split my thumb. Blood began to flow heavily from the wound. Then Mother screamed at me to get out.

It was 3 a.m. in the winter and very cold. I wrapped my hand in a washcloth to try to hold the thumb together and stop the bleeding. The pain was awful. I put on my coat and walked to the bus stop, which was about one-half mile from where I lived. I was the only one on the street that morning and I was scared. I waited what seemed like a very long time before the bus finally arrived. Buses did not run frequently that time of morning.

When the bus finally came, it was empty except for the driver. He asked what a little girl like me was doing out at that time of night. He said, "Little girl, don't you know that nice little girls are at home in bed this time of night? Do your parents know that you are out in the streets this late?"

I answered, "My mother put me out and I am trying to get to my aunt's house so that she can take me to the hospital. I hurt my hand." I was too ashamed to tell the bus driver that my mother had hurt me.

The driver asked, "Your parents put you out this time of night, why?"

"Because they don't want me no more. Please, can you take me to my Aunt Maelizzie's house?"

He asked me where she lived and I told him, "603 Third Avenue, but I ain't got no money to pay you."

Then he saw the blood-soaked rag on my finger and said in a concerned voice, "Sweetheart, you're hurt. You don't have any business trying to ride a bus. It looks to me like you should be seeing a doctor. I'll get you a taxi and pay the fare for you to go to the hospital. You need medical help. What I should do is call the police. I think someone hurt you and you don't want to tell me who it was. But I suspect it was probably one of your parents. Am I right?"

I got scared and begged him please not to call the police. I didn't want my mother to go to jail. I started crying and said to the driver, "Please Mister, my mother really does love me. She didn't mean to hurt me. She just gets mad sometimes and doesn't know what she's doing. When she gets sober, she is going to be sorry that she hurt me, watch."

The kind driver said, "Un, huh, I figured something like that happened. I didn't think you had hurt yourself. But if I ever see you like his again, I will have to call the police. I have a little girl just about your age and I don't think children should be hurt."

He got off the bus and stopped a taxi for me and gave the taxi driver some money and told him to take me to my aunt's house. I had wakened Maelizzie at this time of night and she was very upset with me. She began to scold me. She was oblivious to my pain. She didn't want me to stay at her house and she wouldn't take me to the hospital. She turned her anger to Mother by saying how no good my mother was and that she was just an old drunk who didn't have any business having any children.

After she had said all she wanted to say and her anger was satisfied to an extent, she made a pallet on the front room floor for me to sleep. There was an extra bed in there but she didn't want me to sleep in it. I lay on the floor and cried all night. I was afraid that Maelizzie would hear me, so I put the bed sheet into my mouth to muffle the sobs. My finger throbbed and ached all night and the pain would not let me sleep.

The next day my Uncle Bob gave me a dime for bus fare to ride home. By then my thumb had swollen badly and was hurting something awful. The blood had dried around the wound and the finger had turned dark. Maelizzie never asked me about my finger, and she didn't give me breakfast before I left for home. She just told me to clean up the mess in the front room before I left, which meant to put away the sheets and pillow used as a pallet. I rode the bus home trying to hide my hand from the people on the bus.

When I got home, Mother didn't remember hitting me. When I showed her my swollen finger, she began to cry and rushed me to the hospital. The doctor cleaned the wound and put stitches in my finger to close the wound. Mother hugged me and said she was sorry and promised it would not happen again. She was always apologizing when she was sober and I believed her.

About two months after that night Mother came home after she had been drinking and woke me. She insisted I get up to make a fire in the stove. It was very late and we had forgotten to bring in the coal for the next morning's fire. Mother told me to go to the coal house under our house, and get some coal.

I was afraid because the coal house was infested with large insects that resembled giant spiders. They were about the size of a half dollar, had very long legs and could jump very high. They were so large that after they jumped, you could hear them land on the floor. We never did find out what they were or how they came to be in our coal house. In the day time we could see them, but at night in the dark it was very hard to see them because they were black like coal.

I began to cry, saying that I was afraid. Mother insisted that because I was the oldest, I should be the one to go. I began to cry harder and that angered Mother. She picked up the fire poker and tried to hit me in the head with it. I put up my hand to protect my head and the poker struck my hand. I heard the bone in my wrist crack and the pain shot up my arm and my arm went limp. I screamed and said, "Mother, you broke my arm." She called me a faker and tried to hit me again.

I couldn't protect myself that time and Sandy grabbed the poker from Mother and said, "You ain't gonna hit her no more. You did enough to her already." Sandy helped me put on my clothes , because I couldn't raise my arm. I used some of my babysitting money and went to the hospital alone. The doctor put a splint on my arm and wrapped it. When he asked me what happened I lied and said I fell.

Growing

Up Scared

When we bought the house in East Wynnton, we lived on Coolidge Avenue. The house had remained empty and locked up during the year we lived in Trenton. The Thompson family lived next door to us on the right and the Anderson family lived to the left of us.

The Andersons had two small sons and two daughters. The sons were six and seven years old when they moved into the house. Their daughters were born after they had been living there a few years. We had been living in our house before the Andersons moved in.

Mr. Anderson had lived in the house with his mother after he and his first wife, Christine, had divorced. His second wife, Josephine, had two boys from a previous marriage. Years later, the youngest son, Morris, ran away from home because Mr. Anderson was so mean to the boys. He would beat them the same way Frank beat us, but he didn't beat the girls, who were his own children. When he beat the boys they screamed, and Mr. Anderson laughed.

One day when I was at home alone, Mr. Anderson made a pass

at me. He said he had been noticing me a long time and asked me if he could take me out and show me a good time. I was about fifteen years old at the time and I told Mother about it. She confronted him and an argument ensued. I thought they were going to come to blows. The Andersons stopped speaking to us after that incident.

When I saw Mr. Anderson at the movies one Saturday afternoon with a male companion, the companion spoke to me and said, "Hey little girl, you sure is fine."

Mr. Anderson interrupted his friend and said, "Naw man, leave that alone. That's jail bait. She'll tell her mama cause she told on me. I tried to git some of dat." I often saw Mr. Anderson out with other women.

The Thompson family had a younger son, Leroy; a daughter, Sarah, who was my age; twins, Mat and Matthew; Patsy, who was in her twenties; an older daughter, Mary, and an older son, George Robert, who was in his thirties and away in prison.

Because we children were around the same age and because of the proximity of our houses, our families should have been more friendly, but we were not. In fact, the Thompsons and our family feuded for many years, because of a fight between Mother, Mrs. Thompson, and the oldest daughter Mary over some remarks Mother had made about the Thompson family when she was drunk.

There was a rumor that one of the Thompson girls had secretly given birth to a baby out of wedlock and when Mother was drinking one day, she told the entire neighborhood about it.

Mother stood on our front porch one afternoon and yelled as loudly as she could, "All you niggas think you are better than me because I drink liquor. Well some of your husbands pay for my liquor. I ain't no hypocrite. Yes, I drink liquor. I don't pretend to be what I ain't. All ya'll got skeletons in your closets." Then she proceeded to tell everything bad that she knew about all of the neighbors. She talked about the Thompsons, whose son just came home from prison, and about old lady Thompson who drank but didn't want her church folks to know.

Mother also talked about the couple across the street where the husband was a homosexual. She talked about the Whitakers down the street saying that Mr. Whitaker was the man who was always paying for her drinks, because he wanted to have an affair with her, although Mother didn't want him. She talked about the Burke family and about Mr. Burke having an affair with Mrs. Watkins who lived up the street. I mean Mother was a regular gossip columnist that day. "You learn a lot in liquor houses," Mother said.

I was in the seventh grade at Radcliff when I met George Robert for the first time. Because our houses were so close, it was natural that we would eventually meet. I had never seen him but I often heard the Thompson children talk about their "big brother." One day I saw a strange man sitting on the Thompsons' front porch talking to the twins, and to Leroy and Sarah. He was telling them stories. They were laughing and having a good time. I heard one of the twins call him by name and I knew he was George Robert.

Sarah Thompson had told me how well George Robert could write. She said he had written songs, poems, jokes, and some short stories. Because I was the editor of the school paper, I asked him if he would write some jokes for my column and he agreed.

Years later when I became an adult and worked inside a prison with male inmates for a number of years, I learned that quite a few inmates develop or "discover" a talent for writing, drawing and\or composing. Maybe it's because they finally have the time to "find" themselves.

A couple of days after I had asked George Robert to write the jokes, he gave me a pad and said, "Here is what I promised you, but I'm afraid that you won't find it much of a joke." I didn't know what he meant; I just smiled and took the pad. When I went into the house to read what I thought were jokes, I discovered that George Robert had written a love letter telling me how much he wanted to make love to me.

I was flattered, because George Robert was a very good-looking man with a kind of rugged excitement about him. I didn't tell anyone about the letter except my best friend, Janie. After that, he flirted with me every time he saw me and I returned the flirtations. However, I always managed not to be alone with him out of fear of the vast difference in our ages and because he had been in jail.

Radcliff was where I met Carrie Rossiter, who was to become my second best friend. Carrie was very smart in school and I was always trying to compete with her academically. When it was time to leave Radcliff, because it only went to the seventh grade, Carrie was the highest honor student at the school. I was the second highest, and a boy named Jerry Walker was the third highest.

Every time a student made the honor roll at Radcliff, the teacher would write the student's name on the blackboard in a reserved area call the "HONOR CORNER." If the student didn't make the honor roll the following six weeks, his or her name was erased. Because Carrie and I made the honor roll every six weeks, our names stayed on the board so long that when we were leaving Radcliff transferring to Carver Heights School to begin the eighth grade, the teachers could not wash our names off the board. The chalk that spelled our names had been on the board so long it was imprinted in the blackboard. At that time, the boards were black, not green.

I babysat for the principal of Radcliff almost every weekend. That meant that I had to perform well academically because he was always telling his children that they should try to be just like me.

I always had a very active imagination that became acutely active at Radcliff when I was in Mrs. Bruback's homeroom class. Mrs. Bruback was a short little teacher with coal black, wavy hair and she wore it pulled tightly back from her face in a bun on her neck. She was a rather nice-looking woman but she had a peculiar shape. She was very flat behind, had a large stomach, and tiny legs that did not seem to match her body.

Our classroom was in the annex, which was made up of little shacks on the grounds of the school that served as extra classrooms. The students whose classrooms were in the main building would laugh and tease those of us whose classrooms were in the annex. The cafeteria, library, and principal's office were all in the main building. That meant when it was time to go to the cafeteria, if it was raining, we got wet.

Mrs. Bruback was my homeroom teacher and she also taught history. We were studying medieval history and learning about the Romans, the Greek gods, and the Babylonians. Once when Mrs. Bruback gave the class an assignment for completion at home to be presented and discussed in class the following day, we all either forgot to do the assignment, or simply didn't do it. Mrs. Bruback was furious.

She told us that the entire class would be punished and made to stay after school and complete the projects before we went home that day. She said she didn't care if we had to stay there all night, we were not leaving until we finished our assigned home projects. She also said that she was going to call each one of our parents and tell them why we were kept after school, and because it would be dark when we were allowed to leave school, she was not going to dismiss us until our parents came to get us.

We were real scared because we knew if she called our parents and told them that we had not done our homework, we would be punished, and because our parents would have to come to school to get us, we knew that the punishment would be severe.

I had brought to school a small replica of a Japanese house and other Japanese articles including a parasol, a doll, a pair of Japanese pajamas, a kimono, and so on that Frank had sent to us when he was stationed in Japan. When Mrs. Bruback threatened to call our parents, I raised my hand and said, "Mrs. Bruback, I did my homework last night and I am ready to present it to the class. I didn't say anything when you first asked us abut our projects, because I didn't want to be the first one to show what I had done."

I was lying, of course , because I had not done my project, but I didn't want her to call my parents, especially Frank. I knew what I would get when I got home if I had not done my homework - knowing that I had lied the day before when I wanted to go skating, and had told Mother that I was finished with my homework.

Mrs. Bruback knew I was lying. She said in a loud demanding voice, "O.K., little girl. You march yourself up here in front of the class and give your presentation. It had better be good. If I do not think it is well prepared, I will stop you in the middle of your presentation and the entire class will witness you getting ten licks on your hand with my strap for lying."

Mrs. Bruback's method of whipping was to bend the palm of the hand back as far as it could go and hitting the palm with a strap made by nailing two pieces of thick leather strap to a piece of wood that served as a handle.

I knew Mother would not tolerate my skipping homework and she certainly would not be pleased that I had lied about completing my assigned project. I knew she would listen to what Mrs. Bruback said about my behavior in class; furthermore, had I gotten a spanking in school and had Mrs. Bruback told Mother, I would get another whipping when I got home.

I rose from by seat, took all my Japanese things from the box in which I had carried them to school, and walked slowly to the front of the classroom. I was only two seats from the front of the classroom, but that day it seemed the longest walk I had ever taken. I couldn't remember that walk being so long before. I felt like a condemned prisoner walking the last mile to the electric chair or the gas chamber.

When I started my presentation, I began talking about how all the houses in Japan were built with detachable roofs so that the families could remove the roofs to defend themselves from their enemies. I demonstrated to the class how the roofs were removed by taking the roof from the toy Japanese house I was holding. (I didn't know the roof was removable so that the house could fit inside the shipping box.) I showed pictures of where the parents slept and talked about where the children stayed. I talked about what the Japanese children learned in school. I even contrasted Japanese children to American children.

What I was doing was combining information I read in comic books with information I learned in history class about Japan, and with information that my stepfather had told me about Japan. I told such a good story that Mrs. Bruback did not stop me. Instead, she allowed me to finish. She sat at her desk and seemed quite fascinated with my presentation. When I finished, she asked me, "When did you make up that story, Barbran?" (Everyone called me that. They put my first and middle names together and it came out as one word.)

The expression on her face told me to tell her the truth this time and accept the consequences. I had run out of lies anyway and I didn't know what else to say, so I told her the truth.

"I just made it up as I was walking to the front of the class, Mrs. Bruback, and I just made up the rest as I went along."

She asked, "Why did you try to take it upon yourself to protect the entire class?"

"Because after school we are going to play against Mrs. Powell's class in softball, and I didn't want her class to think we were chicken and that we deliberately didn't show up today for the game because we were afraid of them. They have been bragging all week about how they are going to beat us because they are better than we are. If we are kept after school, we would automatically lose the game."

Mrs. Powell's classroom was in the main building. We were better than they were in softball and we beat them every time we played. We also beat them in volley ball, but they still thought they were better than we were because they were in the main building.

Mrs. Bruback smiled and said to the class, "Barbran saved your ball game. You should all thank her. Because of her presentation, I am not going to make you stay after school. Just remember, the assignments that were due today are due tomorrow. If you do not have your assignments completed for class tomorrow, not only will you stay after school, you will also get ten licks in your hands."

The entire class cheered in unison, because they were so happy. Then Mrs. Bruback said to the class as she looked directly at me, "Wait a minute everybody. Barbran, I want you to know that I did not believe your story, but you told it so well and you were brave enough to get up here and tell it, plus it was such a beautiful story, and the fact that you made it up on the spur of the moment, that I am letting the class go to reward you for having such a vivid and creative imagination."

One day, the president of the Parent-Teacher Association (P.T.A.), Mrs. Parker, decided she wanted Jackie Potts and me to sing a duet at the next P.T.A. meeting. Jackie was a boy in my class who had a beautiful tenor voice. Jackie and I practiced after school for the duet. I was very scared because I knew that I couldn't sing well enough for a group of teachers and parents.

On the night of the P.T.A. meeting, I figured that Mother at least would go, because I wanted her to hear me sing; at least I wanted her to see that I had been chosen to sing. Although I was scared and nervous, I was still proud that they had picked me instead of Carrie or Anita. While I was getting ready to go to school, Mother went out saying that she would be right back. I knew that she would not come right back. I also knew that when she did come back she would have been drinking. I sat and waited for her just the same. I don't know why, but I waited. When she didn't return, I went to the meeting alone.

I knew I would be late, but I didn't care. I cried all the way to the school. I tried to walk slowly so that no one would be able to tell I had been crying. Although I had walked that route literally hundreds of times before, that night, going to the P.T.A. meeting without my mother made the trip take forever.

I didn't know what my answer would be if someone asked me where my parents were. Radcliff was about five miles from where we lived. When I arrived at the school, Jackie had finished singing. Because I was not there, he sang "Love's Old Sweet Song" as a solo. I made up some story about why I was late. All of my friends were there with their mothers. I felt so alone.

Mary Ann Smith, who lived in my neighborhood, was there with her mother. Her mother was a seamstress and she always made Mary Ann and her older sister, Betty Jean, beautiful clothes. For special holidays such as Easter and Mother's Day, my sister and I barely got one new outfit, but Mary Ann's mother made her two and three outfits. Mary Ann would change clothes two and three times on those days just to show off her outfits. She bragged about how many clothes she had and she called our clothes shabby. Sometimes we went home with tears in our eyes. Our clothes were not really shabby. They were not from the best stores but Mother did the best she could.

After the P.T.A. meeting was over, I knew that I would have an adult to go home with. When Mary Ann's mother went to P.T.A. meetings, Mrs. Walker, who lived next door to Mary Ann, went also. Thus, I knew that a lot of parents would be walking home in the direction of our house.

Mrs. Walker was a very large woman. She had seven children. It always amazed us to think of how Mr. and Mrs. Walker and all those children lived in a house that had only two rooms and a kitchen. When the P.T.A. meeting was over, Mrs. Parker was walking in front of the crowd. We had to pass her house to get to Buena Vista Road, which would take us to our neighborhood. All the kids were walking in front of the grown folks. After Mrs. Parker turned into her yard, we all said our good-byes, and spent a few moments discussing the events of the evening and then continued on our way.

The kids and I were walking in a group laughing, telling lies, scaring each other with ghost stories, and just enjoying being out in the star-filled summer night. I had almost forgotten the disappointment of not having my mother with me. I only thought about my being alone when one of the kids would tell a story, then try to convince the rest of us that it was true by getting his or her mother to confirm it. It brought pain to my heart to realize that I was alone.

Beuna Vista Road was the main boulevard in Columbus and very busy. Travelers who wanted to get around Columbus used Buena Vista Road as the center point.. Suddenly, we heard tires squealing and someone shouted, "Look out!" We all stopped and looked around to see what had happened. It was Frank, my stepfather, turning his military police car around in the middle of Buena Vista Road, right in the middle of all the traffic. He wore the military police uniform like a trophy.

He pulled his car over to where I was standing with the rest of the kids and adults and shouted, "Get your ass in this car. I am gonna beat the shit out of you when I git you home."

Mrs. Smith said to Frank, "Beat her for what? She is only walking home from a P.T.A. meeting. She ain't done nothing wrong for you to go and beat her.. She done been wit me all da time she been at da program. We's takin her home. What kin be wrong wid dat?"

Mrs. Smith's mother said, "You wrong, Frank. Dat chil don deserve no beatin. You wrong!"

Frank answered furiously, "She's my damn daughter and you ain't got a damn thing to do wit it. She ain't got no business walking wid no wild boys."

Mrs. Smith said, "But what kin happen wid all us grown folks takin da children home? She ain't wid no little boys, she's wid all of us."

Frank became more angry with each question asked. His large eyes protruded from his head and made him look even more like a bullfrog. The madder he became, the bigger his eyes got. I really thought that he was going to strike Mrs. Smith. He looked at me menacingly and said in a low growl, "I told you to git your ass into dis car. If I have to say it again, I will git out and drag you in here."

I knew that if I did not obey he would take off his belt and beat me in front of everyone. I got into the car and he cursed and threatened me all the way home. I was so scared. I thought, "Surely this time he will kill me. But maybe that's o.k., `cause nobody loves me anyway."

Kids are so cruel without even realizing it. The same group of kids who just minutes before were walking, laughing, and telling jokes with me were now running behind the car, taunting me and following me home so that they could hear me get a beating.

When we got home, Frank took me into the house, got the ironing cord, doubled it, made me take off all my clothes except my underpants and beat me until I had welts all over. He even hit my face and all over my arms as I tried to protect my face by covering it with my arms. While he was beating me he kept telling me how he did not ever want to see me with any little boys again or he would beat me right in front of them.

He beat me until the welts started to bleed. I fell down on my knees and clasped my hands together as in prayer and begged him, "Please don't kill me, Daddy. I won't do it no more. I'll be good." He ignored my pleas and asked me, "Where did you git dat shit from; begging like dat?"

When he began to pant from shortness of breath and sweat from the exertion of beating me, he told me to go to bed. All the kids were outside listening to me screaming and they were laughing at me and mocking me. I heard one of them say in a mocking voice, "Please don't kill me, Daddy." Then they all laughed out loud. They teased me for a long time after that. In my childish mind, I didn't understand why Frank beat me. Later I learned that it was because he was jealous that I was with some boys and that he had feelings for me that were not all fatherly.

Years later when I was in college and visiting my boyfriend who was to later become my husband, Frank said that the reason he was so strict with me and didn't want me to have any boyfriends was because he didn't think that anybody was good enough for me.

Every time Mother and Frank got into an argument, Mother always scored points by insulting him. That is to say that Mother always said something about Frank that sounded comical and Sandy and I would laugh. Frank always tried to "comeback" by making a comment about Mother that was equally as comical, but he never could top her. Even if we thought that what Frank said was funny, we would not laugh. We knew, however, that he wanted us to laugh.

Sandy and I would never laugh at anything he said and that made him angry. Sometimes he tried to hit us when we laughed at what Mother had said, because he was embarrassed, but Mother always protected us from him, whether she was drunk or sober.

If Mother had not been drinking and was arguing with Frank, she could tear him up with words. He couldn't compete with her intellect, wisdom or sense of humor, and he resented that.

Both of them were fighting one night - I mean violently fighting - and Mother's screams woke me up. I knew that she had been drinking by the way she was screaming. I shook Sandy, who was sleeping in the bed beside me, "Sandy, Sandy, wake up. Daddy is hurting Mother again."

Sandy asked, "What are we going to do?"

"We got to help Mother," I replied. We jumped out of bed and ran into Mother's and Frank's bedroom and saw them struggling with a butcher knife. Sandy and I began to cry. Just as we were begging them to stop fighting, Frank cut Mother on her arm with the knife. The knife made a clean cut as if it were cutting soft butter. As the knife went through mother's skin, the flesh separated and before the blood came, I saw white meat where the knife had laid my mother's arm open with a deep, nasty wound.

That night I heard the most chilling scream I had ever heard. It sounded as though it was coming from far away. Someone just kept screaming and screaming. Mother and Frank stopped fighting and looked at me. I wondered why they were looking at me rather than trying to find out where that blood-curdling scream was coming from.

At first I thought it was Mother screaming, but I noticed that she was just standing there bleeding, looking in my direction but her mouth was not open; besides, it was not her voice I was hearing. I didn't recognize the voice. The screams wouldn't stop. They were so loud that they were giving me a headache. I put my hands up to cover my ears, vainly attempting to drown out the screams. Mother ran to me, put her arms around me, and tried to comfort me. I didn't understand why, I just wanted her to make the screams stop.

Then suddenly, I put my hands to my mouth and discovered that it was open. I realized I was the one screaming. I had never heard such a terrifying scream. After the screaming finally stopped, Frank and Mother stopped fighting, for the night anyway. Mother had to go to the hospital that night to get stitches in her arm. The next day she took me to a doctor because I couldn't get rid of the headache from the previous night. I went to the doctor several times but he couldn't stop the headaches.

A few days later, for no apparent reason, I fainted in school. I just passed out, cold. I was walking down the hall and the next thing I knew, I woke up in the hospital. After the doctor examined me, he referred me to a psychiatrist. I was either thirteen or fourteen years old at the time.

It wasn't long before Frank and Mother were fighting again; this time with an ice pick. Frank had the ice pick and I just knew he was going to kill Mother with it. They struggled for the ice pick, but Frank was too strong. He stabbed Mother in the chest and the blood squirted out of the punctured hole. Blood from Mother's wound splashed clear across the room and some of the blood got on me.

Again, I heard the awful screaming. I tried to stop, because the sounds were giving me a terrible headache, but I couldn't control the screams. I made up my mind right then that if Frank ever hit me or my mother again, I would kill him.

I was always a nervous wreck when they fought but once I had made up my mind to kill Frank, a strange calmness came over me. It was as if a weight had been lifted from my shoulders. I felt that I had finally made a decision about something that had been bothering me for a long time. I knew that I would probably go to jail, but I didn't care. It would be worth it if Frank would not be around to hurt my mother anymore.

I gave Sandy my paper dolls and comic books collection and waited for Frank to hit us again so that I could kill him. I didn't know how I was going to do it because then he weighed almost four hundred pounds and stood about six feet tall. I weighed ninety-four pounds and was five feet tall. But I knew I was going to kill him.

I told Janie about my decision to kill Frank. Naturally, she tried to talk me out of it, but I wouldn't listen. The reason I didn't carry out my plan was that before Frank and Mother got into another fight, Mother discovered that she was pregnant. I was disappointed. I couldn't understand why she would want to have another child by a man like Frank.

He still beat her during her pregnancy, and with every blow he gave her he kept swearing and hollering, "You ain't big, you ain't big." Mother drank throughout her entire pregnancy. I couldn't understand how she could love someone who beat her all the time. I decided if that's what love and marriage were all about, I didn't want any part of either.

Before long, my brother Al was born. We wanted to name him Nigel but Frank insisted that Mother name him Alphonza. Mother looked pretty when she was pregnant. By the time Al was born, Sandy had long since stopped caring about school and she had started staying out late at night. Sandy always stayed out when Mother was out drinking and Frank was out with other women so that they wouldn't find out about her.

It would have been so easy for me to hang out in the streets at night. With Mother and Frank out, each doing his and her own thing, I had no one to tell me that I could not go out. Besides, Columbus was an army town, so there were always plenty of good-looking soldiers looking for young girls.

I was a very attractive girl. People told me that I was pretty. I had long hair, deep dimples in my cheeks, slanted eyes, a brown complexion, and a seductive walk. But the only thing that I thought about was going to college and being SOMEBODY. I wanted to get out of the South and go to school up North somewhere, get a good education, find a good job that made a lot of money, buy a nice house, marry a husband who would look only at me, have two children, a boy and a girl, have a successful career, and be happy.

I wouldn't date any married men, although God knows enough of them were after me, including some of the teachers at my school. I had the notion that if I didn't bother another woman's husband while I was growing up, when I got married, God would not let another woman bother mine. How ironic life can be sometimes. As hard as I worked to keep married men out of my life while I was growing up, I eventually married a married man.

Frank and Mother moved their bedroom into the new room that had been added after Al was born. That left the front room, which had been their bedroom, vacant. Finally, we had a living room. I was so glad, because the excuse Frank had always used as to why we couldn't receive male company was that we didn't have a place to entertain them. I didn't believe that, because if it were true, why did he beat me so often when I only walked home or talked with boys? Nevertheless, I was still glad that we had a place we could use for entertaining.

I was home with my baby brother Al one night, when he woke up and began to cry. I didn't know anything about taking care of a baby, yet Mother had breast fed him, laid him on the sofa beside me and left. I didn't know that she had gone out. I thought she was in her bedroom, so when the baby woke up and began to cry, I went to get Mother. When I discovered that she had gone out the back door and that I was alone with the baby, I didn't know what to do.

I picked Al up and put him on my shoulder trying to comfort him. I had heard that sometimes babies need to be burped to help them digest their food and to release air bubbles from their stomachs. I didn't know if that was true, but I wanted to comfort my baby brother.

When I put Al on my shoulder and patted his back, he vomited milk mixed with whisky ingested from nursing from Mother's breast after she had been drinking. I could smell the alcohol in the milk. Probably he had awakened crying because his stomach was hurting. He was usually such a good baby so it was unusual for him to wake up crying. I didn't know what to do, or how to comfort him. I just sat and held him and cried with him.

I cried because I was scared. I cried because my poor little helpless, beautiful curly-headed brother had to be born into a family such as ours. I cried because I didn't know how to help him and I didn't know how to help myself. I cried because everyone in my mother's family seemed to worry about their own selfish problems, and no one seemed to give a damn about the fact I was being abused and that now my precious little baby brother was being neglected. I cried because we were alone. I cried because there was nothing else to do.

I finally got the baby back to sleep. I sat on the sofa that faced the fireplace in the living room and watched the flames dance up the chimney as they turned blue, red, yellow, and orange, and made eerie shadows on the wall, and I prayed that the baby wouldn't wake up anymore that night. He was so cute and I was so proud that he was my brother.

Sandy and I never thought of ourselves as half-sisters, and I certainly never thought of Al as my half-brother. We felt as one family and we resented anyone saying anything to the contrary. Oh sure, we fought among ourselves as most siblings do, but we dared anyone else to hit either of us. We were always fighting for each other.

While Al lay on the sofa beside me sleeping, I patted him on his back. The fire was so relaxing. After a while I forgot about how scared I had been and I was just glad that Al had me to take care of him. I made a silent promise to him that I would never let anyone hurt him and that I would rush home from school everyday to take care of him.

As I sat, I mentally began to plan a party for the following week. Such parties were called, Silver Tea Parties because the guests were charged either ten or fifteen cents to attend. Someone gave a party almost every weekend. I had planned to have mine the following week.

While cleaning our bedroom that day, I found a bottle of corn liquor hidden in our clothes closet behind the dirty clothes bag. I knew Mother had hidden it and I also knew that it was corn liquor. I had been around enough to be able to recognize it just by smell. Besides, so many people in my neighborhood not only sold it, some of them also made it.

Many times I had to go into those liquor houses to get my mother. I had become so accustomed to the smell of corn liquor that when Mother was sleeping after she had been drinking, I could tell by her breath if she had been drinking commercial whisky or corn liquor. I didn't even have to be close to her to smell it. I could walk into the room where she lay and the smell of alcohol seemed to come from the pores of her skin.

Anyway, I found her bottle of liquor and the idea came to me. I would hide the bottle until my party, then I would use the liquor to spike the punch. I knew that no one would be at home to tell me that I couldn't do it, because on the weekends Sandy and I were usually on our own.

When the night of the party finally came, I waited until Frank had dressed and gone before I began cleaning the house for the party. Mother didn't come home from work and that usually meant that she would be drunk when she did come home. I silently hoped that the party would be over and my friends gone by the time Mother came home.

She had always worked as a presser in a dry cleaners and she was very good at it. She didn't ever worry about being fired, because she was in such great demand. It seemed that all the major cleaners in Alex City and Columbus knew that Mother was the best presser around.

She could quit, or not go to work, or get drunk, or curse out her boss, or leave for lunch and never return to work that day, yet, she would still have her job the following day. I had seen her quit a job and the owner would rehire her whenever she went back. She was good, real good. After she went on a drinking binge, which was often, her employer would take her back saying, "She is the best at what she does and her drinking doesn't take that away from her. She can finish more clothes in better condition in three hours than the other pressers can in one day. Plus, your mama ain't no dummy."

After I finished cleaning, I made sandwiches of bologna, mayonnaise and cheese, and put potato chips in bowls and set them on the lamp tables for my guests. I had purchased the refreshments with money I earned babysitting.

Al was asleep and Sandy had dressed and gone wherever it was she went every night when she had the chance, which was practically every weekend. I didn't care where she was. I was selfish and glad to have the house all to myself for my party. I figured that I could take care of the baby. He really wasn't much trouble, because he didn't cry much.

He was such a good baby, such a happy baby, always smiling all over his little toothless, curly headed face. I would tease him and call him my little "toothless old man" and he would just laugh. I knew he didn't understand what I was saying because he was only five or six months old, but he must have sensed that the sound of my voice meant," I love you."

I began making the punch. I had bought large bottles of soda called, Par-T-Pak and I went into the clothes closet looking for the bottle of corn liquor that I had hidden. The bottle was not where I had put it. I took every single, solitary thing out of that closet looking for that bottle, but it was nowhere to be found. I was so disappointed I felt like crying. Then I realized, Mother must have found the bottle and emptied it. Why not? She had hidden it in the first place.

The joke was on me. I had bragged to my friends all week that I would be serving spiked punch, now I couldn't fulfill my boast. I wondered how I would explain it to my guests. I knew for a fact a lot of the boys from school were coming only because I had said I would be serving alcoholic punch. I decided to lie; I would say that my little sister stole the whisky and gave it to her boyfriend. One could always blame a younger sister or brother when things went wrong.

Two Women

Everyone at school was talking about the movie, *The Greatest Story Ever Told*, a religious picture. I wanted to go but Mother didn't have the money and I knew we could not afford it. I tried to hide my disappointment but Mother caught me crying. When she saw how much going to that movie meant to me, she gave me the money she had been saving to buy herself a pair of shoes for work.

I didn't want to take the money because I knew how badly she needed those shoes. The soles were coming off the pair she was wearing, nevertheless she insisted that I take the money and go to the movie. She was a proud woman and she didn't want people to think that she couldn't afford to send me to the movie with my friends.

She tied a string around the shoes she was wearing to hold the soles on and she wore those shoes until she could afford a new pair. I loved her for that. That was the way she was; she was my mother.

There were two windows that led from the front porch into the living room. The windows were so low that a person could get into the living room simply by stepping through the windows from the front porch. When Mother and Frank finally could afford to renovate the house, they decided to have the two small windows made into one large picture window. When the contractors came to install the new window, they couldn't finish the job the same day. They were to return the following day to complete the installation.

Rather than securing the area where the two small windows had been, the contractors simply left a large, gaping hole where the new window was to go. We had to sleep that night with a hole in the front wall. Mother put a bed sheet over it to give us some privacy from the street.

I don't remember where Frank was at the time, I just remember that he wasn't at home. Mother was concerned about the opening, but not overly afraid since our house stood in a row of twelve other houses that were so close together a person could literally jump from one porch to the other straight down the line of houses.

Nevertheless, Mother saw how scared Sandy and I were about the windowpane not being there, so she decided to bring the baby and sleep with us in our bed. Mother said that I tossed and turned all night and the bed was not large enough for all four of us to sleep comfortably. She decided to make a pallet on the floor beside our bed, and she and the baby slept there while Sandy and I shared the bed. She used two of Mama's handmade quilts and the pillow from her bed to make up the pallet.

I don't know why I woke in the middle of the night, but thank God that I did, because I saw a figure standing over Mother as she lay sleeping on the floor. It was the figure of a man with a cap on his head, standing straddled over Mother, looking down at her. At first I thought it was my sister Sandy, because my eyes had to adjust to the darkness. I rubbed my eyes and asked, "Sandy, is that you?"

With that, the man ran. The noise he made while running through the house woke Mother. He must have stumbled over some furniture, because we heard a loud noise as if he had fallen. Mother sat up and asked what the noise was. I told her what I had seen, and then we heard the man run into the front room, jump through the window onto the porch, and jump from the porch onto the ground.

We were so scared. Between sobs I was trying to tell Mother what had happened. As I was talking, we heard someone whistle and someone else answer with another whistle. It seemed that two people were signaling to each other. Through neighborhood gossip, we later heard that one of the men who lived down the street liked Mother, but she wasn't interested in him. He thought that Mother was drunk that night and he had planned to rape her.

His plan was spoiled when Mother decided to sleep in our room rather than in her bed with the baby. His plan was complicated further by Mother being sober, and to make matters worse for him, I surprised him by waking up and seeing him. We also heard that the person who was returning the whistle was the lookout in case he spotted Frank's car coming. I thank God for allowing me to wake up when I did.

Mother was so drunk one day that she drove Frank's car to school to get me. She couldn't drive and she didn't have a driver's license. The booze told her that she should drive to school to get her daughter. Frank's car was parked outside our house and she got behind the wheel and started to drive. God knows how she managed to get to the school without an accident. The school was about five miles from our house and we had to go through the white folks' section of East Wynnton, across a very busy boulevard. I was sitting in class when I heard a crash. My classmates heard it too.

Spencer High was a new school that the white folks built for us "Negro children" so that we would be satisfied with our own school and wouldn't try to integrate their schools. The issue of desegregation of schools in the South was just surfacing. Spencer was a beautiful school with all the modern innovations possible in the early fifties. One side of each classroom was entirely windows. The driveway was circular and was in full view of all the classrooms, which were on that side of the school.

When I saw the car and the way it swerved around the corner of the circular driveway with the wheels making all that noise, I knew instantly that Mother had been drinking. Even before she got out of the car, barely able to stand, I knew. I hoped the students who had a clear view of the driveway wouldn't notice, but they did. When I saw that she had hit someone's car parked in the driveway, I hoped it didn't belong to a parent, but it did.

The woman got out of her car and proceeded to argue with Mother. I jumped from my seat and ran out of the classroom to go and get Mother before she embarrassed herself and me by getting into a fight with the woman. I knew that if they stood there and argued long enough, Mother would get angry enough to hit her and, because Mother had been drinking, she was not in any condition to defend herself. The woman was very angry and was shouting at Mother when I arrived.

I heard her say to Mother, "You drunken bum, this is my husband's car you just hit."

Mother looked the woman straight in the eye and said with indignation, "I may be drunk, but I ain't no bum. Hell, this is my husband's car too. You're not the only one with a husband." If it wasn't so embarrassing with almost the entire school looking, it would have been funny. Mother ended the argument with a promise to pay for the damages if the woman wouldn't call the police.

I persuaded Mother to get into the car and let me drive her home. I didn't have a driver's license either, but I could drive a little. I was certainly in better condition to drive than she was, I reasoned. I just took the chance that the police wouldn't stop me before I got home. I didn't bother to tell my teacher that I was leaving the school, as we were required to do. I just wanted to get Mother home. The teachers knew anyway, because the driveway was directly outside the principal's office.

I cried all the way home, but it didn't seem to bother Mother that she had embarrassed me. I was too young to view alcoholism as a disease. I just knew that I didn't like it when my mother got drunk. Later in life I learned how addicts and alcoholics think and about their behavior patterns. I wish I had known more about alcoholism when I was growing up.

When I got the car in front of our house, before I could park it, Mother jumped out and went looking for something more to drink. I walked up the street to be alone. I couldn't go back to school to face the teasing from my schoolmates and the pitying looks from teachers.

Mother never did honor her promise to pay the woman for the damage she had done to the car. Mother said that because she had not given the woman her address, she probably would never see her again. However, as I will explain later, eventually her assumption was proven wrong.

My grandmother had been suffering from diabetes for a long time. Her condition got progressively worse until finally it was necessary to put her in the hospital. The hospitals in Alabama discriminated against black people in those days. Just as there were separate toilets, drinking fountains, and eating areas in stores and other public facilities such as service stations, bus stations, and train stations, there were also separate areas in hospitals that were designated for colored people, and the quality of the treatment was considerably inferior to the treatment given to white patients. Some doctors flatly refused to treat colored patients.

The colored areas of the hospitals were filthy. The doctors and nurses, including some colored doctors and nurses, mistreated the sick, colored patients so badly and the facilities for colored patients were of such poor quality, that it was necessary to send Mama to a hospital outside of Alexander City. Mother, my Aunt Maelizzie, Sandy, Frank, baby Al, and I went to visit Mama when she was in the hospital. Because Al was too young, the nurse would not let us take him upstairs to the ward to visit Mama. That hurt us very badly, because Mama had never seen Al. I was always very emotional, especially about someone whom I cared for as much as I cared about my grandmother.

When I saw Mama lying in the hospital bed so helpless, I began to cry uncontrollably. Mother and my aunt had to take me out of the hospital. I kept hugging Mama's neck and telling her how much I loved her. Somehow I knew that I would never see her alive again. I cried all the way home. I kept saying over and over, "Mama will never get to see Al. Mama will never get to see Al."

In less than a week, we received a call from the hospital telling us Mama had died. Since we still didn't have a telephone, the call came to Mrs. Marie's, who lived across the street from us.

Once, we did have a telephone but Frank wouldn't pay the phone bill, and the telephone company cut off service. For a long time the disconnected phone just sat in the front room. Then, one day I came home from school and saw the telephone company's truck parked in front of our house. I was so happy. I thought they had come to re-connect our phone; instead, they had come to remove it. We were the only family in the neighborhood who didn't have a telephone.

When Mrs. Marie called Mother and told her there was an emergency long distance call from the hospital, I knew in my heart that it was to tell us that Mama had died. I sat on the front steps and waited for Mother to come back. When she did, she was crying and I knew. Without her saying a word, I knew. Mother put her arms around me and said between sobs, "We've lost Mama, Baby. Mama is gone."

I said between sobs, "I know I am going to finish school now." Mama had always told me that no matter what happened, just graduate from high school. She had not had the opportunity to go to school and neither had my mother. I was to be the first in my family to graduate from high school and the first to go to college. Mama always told me that it was up to me to be whatever I wanted to be.

She would say, "Barbran, you are going to make Mama so proud of you. You are going to be somebody important and Mama is going to be sitting there smiling saying, `that's my baby, that's my granddaughter.' You might not be able to see me, but I'll be there, sitting right up front. I don't want you to be sad cause you can't see me. I want you to be happy cause you done made yo Mama mighty proud."

I was in the tenth grade when Mama died and from that day on, I made up my mind that God was the only one who would prevent me from graduating from school. Although times were very hard for me when I was growing up, I had promised my sweet, loving grandmother that I would finish school and nothing this side of hell would prevent me from fulfilling that promise. I didn't know how I was going to college, I just knew I would. I didn't even know how I was going to finish high school, I just knew I would.

I also knew that I would never forget my seventh grade teacher's words. She had said, "Young lady, you will never finish school. In fact, I doubt that you will ever make it to the ninth grade." The only reason she said that was because of my home situation, which was widely known. Everyone believed that I was promiscuous and was having sex with a lot of boys and soldiers. They thought, because they saw my parents out doing their thing and they knew that I had a lot of unsupervised time on my hands, that I was out sleeping with soldiers.

But the truth was, I wasn't doing anything like that. I knew that I wanted to go to college and I was afraid of getting pregnant. My grandmother had told me that it was up to me to be whatever I wanted to be and I believed her. So, I didn't care what anyone thought or said about me. I knew that Mama was somewhere in heaven looking down on me and she believed in me even if no one else did, and I believed in myself. The day Mama died I made a vow to her and to myself. I fell to my knees and said in a whisper so no one else could hear, "Mama, I know you are up there looking at me. I promise you that I will finish school and graduate with honors."

Getting My Act Together

I have always worked. I have had a job since I was in the seventh grade. I guess that is one of the lessons I learned from my mother. She always said, "Hard work never hurt nobody. Always work for what you get and you will appreciate it more. Never touch what does not belong to you. I hate a liar and a thief." She was right.

I was cured very early of trying to steal. Once Janie and I went to the five-and-dime store. Janie dared me to steal a tube of glue. I started to put it into my pocket, but because of my nervousness, I squeezed the tube too hard and the glue squirted out the bottom. Just at that moment a bell rang and sounded all over the store and I thought it was the store manager calling the police. I didn't know they were ringing the bell to signal to the customers and the employees that it was time for the store to close. My heart did a tap dance and landed in my mouth. I was scared to death.

I dropped the tube and ran for the front door. Just as I reached it, the guard was locking up, which further added to my fear. I thought he was trying to keep me inside until the police arrived. I began to scream and cry. I said, "My mother will pay for the glue. I know you have my fingerprints on the tube. I'm too young to go to jail. I promise I'll never do it again. I'll never even come into this store again if you just let me go home." By that time I was so scared that I wet my panties. Urine was running down my legs, my nose was running, and I was shaking so hard I couldn't stop.

The guard had no idea what I was talking about. By the time he calmed me down enough to make sense out of what I was saying, he laughed so hard tears ran down his cheeks. He told me the reason the bell was ringing, and then he gave me a lecture about not playing inside stores and destroying property that didn't belong to me. He didn't make me pay for the glue, he just sent me home with a warning. I will never forget that day as long as I live.

I had a job babysitting for a white family named Cook. I took the job for the summer to earn money for new school clothes for the fall. That was the way Janie and I got new clothes each year. Mr. and Mrs. Cook tried to convince me to quit school and work for them full time. They were always telling me how many pretty clothes I could buy for myself if I worked full time babysitting and cleaning their house, and, oh yeah, getting their children off to school each day.

Wasn't that ironic? I should quit school to get someone else's children to school. They paid me $10.00 a week. They thought they were being very generous, and they were willing to increase it to $19.00 per week if I quit school and worked for them full time. Big deal!

I quit working for the Cooks and took a job working in a diner that stood in a trailer park quite a distance from school, but I walked to work just the same because I couldn't afford bus fare. The diner was owned and operated by an old white couple who were alcoholics. The woman, Ruth, weighed about ninety-five pounds and stood approximately five feet tall. Her husband, Pinky, weighed about 500 pounds and stood approximately six feet tall. They were a comical couple. The diner was a converted trailer. The trailer park was occupied by white people.

I had to be at work at 3 p.m. but didn't get out of school until 3:45 p.m. That meant that I had to leave school early every day to get to work on time. I had to work until 12 a.m. which meant that either I had to walk home alone at midnight (which I did on numerous occasions because I couldn't afford a cab and the buses didn't go into my neighborhood) or arrange for someone to come and get me when I got off work. However, that was unlikely considering that most of my friends didn't have cars, and those who did were not coming to pick me up every night, some nights maybe, but not every night.

Working at night also meant that I couldn't go to the library and study as often as I needed too. Not being able to visit the library resulted in my grades dropping. On Sundays, when I wasn't working, the library was closed. But, I needed the money.

One day when I was cleaning the coffee pot and changing the water in it, I noticed that water was running down the floor where I was standing. I thought the coffee pot was leaking. I examined it looking for a hole, but then I discovered that the water was not coming from the pot. Instead, it was coming from the stool where Ruth was sitting. I realized that she was calmly sitting there urinating in her clothes while carrying on a conversation with a customer as if nothing were happening.

She turned her head and looked at me as if daring me to say anything, then she turned back and resumed her conversation. The counter stood between her and the customer so he couldn't see that Ruth was pissing on herself. I was behind the counter so I could see it all. I was shocked and couldn't believe my eyes. After the customer left, Miss Ruth told me to get a mop and said, "Mop up this mess." I refused. She told me that she was going to fire me if I didn't mop it up.

I said, "Fire me, and I'll tell everybody the reason I was fired." I lied, because I didn't have any idea whom to tell. I didn't know anyone who knew her, but the bluff worked because, in her drunken stupor, she believed me and mopped it up herself. Another woman, Elsy, was hired later and worked with me in the diner. Elsy was about two years older than I and very attractive, but she was afraid of losing her job. That meant that she was afraid of Pinky and Miss Ruth and would do anything she was told.

Ruth worked in the grill during the day and Pinky worked nights. When Pinky came to work, Ruth would go home and take Elsy with her so that Elsy could clean Ruth's house. Ruth tried to get me to go home with her one night, but I refused. I told her that I was hired as a short order cook, not to be her maid. After that, she didn't bother me about going home with her, but she insisted that Elsy go every night. Elsy said that Ruth just got drunk and slept with her dog. Elsy swore that Ruth was having sex with her dog.

One night at the diner, I heard a scratching at the back kitchen window. I looked up and saw a young white man standing in the window smiling and looking at me. The window was high up on the diner wall which meant that the man had to be standing on something to look inside. Later we found that he had been standing on empty chicken crates. He looked to be in his late twenties or early thirties and he was not bad looking, in fact, he was rather handsome.

He stood there smiling, looking at me and not saying anything. Ruth and Elsy had gone for the night, and that left Pinky and me at the diner. There was a half-door separating the kitchen from the counter where the cash register stood and where Pinky and Ruth both sat on high stools. Whenever they wanted to talk to us, they would lean on the half-door. That was where we put orders for them to pick up.

After a few long moments of silence, the young man said in a whisper so that Pinky couldn't hear, "You know, you are a pretty girl and I want to take you out."

I was afraid, because I had heard so many stories about how white men raped young colored girls. I said in a trembling voice, "I don't have time to go out. I work all the time and when I am not working, I am in school. Anyway, my parents do not permit me to date."

That didn't discourage him. He said, "We don't have to let anybody know. I want to give you nice things and make you feel good. I got some money. I can buy you nice things, lots of pretty clothes. See, I'm not lying."

He then threw a dollar bill through the window and it landed on the floor. That really made me angry. I didn't say a word. I left it on the floor. I didn't make a move to pick it up. I didn't look up. I could have used the money because I was only making fifteen dollars a week. Instead, I snapped, "I do not want or need your money and it will stay on the floor until it rots."

As soon as I spoke the words, Pinky looked into the kitchen and saw the dollar laying on the floor and he asked me who it belonged to. I told him what had happened. The man at the window was gone. As soon as Pinky spoke, I heard whatever the man had been standing on fall, and then I heard running footsteps.

"Give it to me," Pinky said, reaching out his fat hand for the dollar. "If you don't want it, I do," he said grinning.

I said in an angry voice, "I told him when he threw it on the floor that I would not touch it and I meant it. If you want it, you have to come in here and pick it up yourself." Pinky didn't see that as insubordination. All he could see was money on the floor and he rushed his 500 pounds into the kitchen, picked up the dollar, and went back into the diner without another word.

After a while my school grades began to get so bad that I had to quit working at the diner. It was important to earn money that last year of school, because I had to pay graduation expenses, such as my senior year book, class ring, senior dues, prom gown, and Senior Day dress, so I had a number of little jobs that school year.

I worked for a family named Frye. The father worked for a company that made woolen cloth. One day he brought home a unique tweed weave that he had made for his wife. She was very proud of the cloth and believed that she was the only person in the whole world who had that particular design. After Mr. Frye created the design for her, he destroyed the pattern.

When I worked for the Fryes, I learned how to prepare lunch out of almost anything - like making a sandwich of pineapple and mayonnaise on two slices of bread, mixing raisins and mayonnaise and toasting it on a grill, making a sandwich of bananas and mayonnaise or mixing raisins and peanut butter. I didn't work very long for them. They wanted me to quit school and work full time for them as their maid.

The white folks seemed to think that Blacks didn't need to get an education. They thought that we should be satisfied with our lot. Hell, I wanted to get a good education and a good paying profession and take care of myself. I had too many high hopes and plans for my future to stop and spend my life cleaning up after white folks and taking care of their children.

While I was working for the Fryes, I had a night off and my best friend Janie and I had dates with two soldiers whom we had just met. I wanted to go out that night, but Frank didn't allow me to date. I decided that, regardless of the consequences, he was not going to continue to make my life miserable, so Janie and I tried to think of a way I could get out of the house so that we could keep our dates.

I told Frank that I had to babysit for the Fryes that night. I got dressed and put another pair of shoes and make-up into my pocketbook so that I could change for my date. I never did wear much make-up, only a little lipstick and nut brown face powder. As I was preparing to leave, Frank insisted that he drive me to work. I got scared and didn't know what to do. I knew that I couldn't admit that I had lied and felt that I had to follow through with the lie.

During the ride to the Fryes house I kept thinking about what I was going to say when I arrived. When Frank pulled in front of their house Mr. and Mrs. Frye and the children were sitting on the front porch trying to keep cool in the hot, muggy Georgia summer night. I said good-bye to Frank as I hurried out of the car and ran up the pavement to the Fryes front porch. Frank remained parked there for what seemed an eternity. Perhaps it was only a few minutes, but it looked as if he would never leave.

I began to get nervous and wondered if he could tell that I had been lying. What if he had called the Fryes and they told him that I wasn't scheduled to babysit for them that night? Perhaps he just wanted to trick me so that he could have an excuse to beat me again. I was worried. When I reached the porch, I was sweating as though someone had thrown a bucket of water on me. I tried to be nonchalant.

I made small talk with Mr. and Mrs. Frye about it being a hot summer night with not enough air stirring. We talked about nothing in particular and I had to keep busy so as not to show my fear. I was trying to stall for time until Frank left. When he finally drove away, it became apparent to me that Mr. and Mrs. Frye were uneasy with me being there on a night when I was not scheduled.

It never occurred to me that they were uneasy because I was a Black in an all-white neighborhood without a reason. Later when Janie and I laughed about it, we realized that white people naturally think that Blacks are thieves who will harm them or rob them; they thought that was natural.

I ignored their uneasiness and said matter-of-factly, "I came to babysit. What time will you be leaving?" Had they decided to go out because I was already there, I would have died.

Mrs. Frye said, "Babysit? You are not supposed to babysit tonight." She was a typical southern white woman and she spoke with a long southern drawl.

I replied, trying to sound astonished, "But didn't you call me and ask me if I could babysit tonight? That is the reason my father brought me up here."

"Someone is obviously playing a joke and I don't like it. We don't have plans to go out tonight."

"That's o.k. I'll just go back home. I think it was probably one of my friends."

Mr. Frye offered to call my father to let him know that I was on my way home. I asked him please not to as it was a beautiful night and I wanted to walk home. "And besides," I said, "my father has to go to work tonight and if he has to come right back to get me he will be very angry."

Mr. Frye didn't call Frank, but I got the feeling that he began to think I was lying. It wasn't anything he had said; rather, it was the funny expression that came over his face when I told him I wanted to walk home. I guess that because just a few moments earlier I had been complaining about how hot the night was with no air stirring, and now I was saying I wanted to walk home in the "beautiful night air," added to his mistrust and disbelief.

Janie and the two soldiers met me on the corner. (They were parked just around the corner from the Fryes.) I got into the car and we laughed about how we had put one over on Frank. We went to pick up two more of our friends. We figured there was safety in numbers.

We visited the NCO Club that night, danced, and tried to act grown-up. We didn't stay out late, nor did we drink alcohol. Some of the more popular girls at school had formed a club, the Tap Tap Club. The members were girls who "went all the way" with boys. The members often came to school after they had been with a boy the previous night, and talked about how they "watched the stars last night." That meant they had been lying on their backs having sex.

Janie and I wanted to become members, so we talked like that too. But they didn't believe us. We were considered outsiders because we didn't visit the army post and frequent the NCO Club every weekend

with them. But everyone just naturally assumed we were promiscuous, because we were always on the go. Frank thought so and so did
Janie's father.

When my sister Sandy got pregnant in the eleventh grade, Frank
blamed me. He said that the only reason I didn't get pregnant was
because I made the boys wear "rubbers." But that was not true. Janie's
father called us "Road Hawks," because we were always going somewhere. Janie and I were too busy having fun to think about sex.
Besides, we never stayed with a boy long enough to get serious.

I took a job babysitting for another woman whose name I cannot
remember. She had a complex about how babysitters or "Mothers's
helpers," as some of the white folks called us, were supposed to dress.
Her husband always picked me up at my house and drove me to their
house whenever they wanted me to babysit. I always dressed as nice
as I could afford too. We were not a middle-class family by any stretch
of the imagination. In fact, we were not even lower middle class.

I began to dress well when I was old enough to work and earn
money to purchase my own clothes. I knew that Mother couldn't
afford to buy me the kind of clothes I saw in magazines. The only time
we got new clothes was for special occasions such as Christmas,
Easter, Mother's Day, and one new outfit to wear on the first day of
school.

I don't know why, but it was a tradition that children would get
new outfits for Mother's Day. We put on our new clothes and wore
a red rose if our mother was living and a white rose if she was not.
That was the way it was in the South, "in the olden days," as my
children say. It sounds as if it were so long ago when my children refer
to my childhood, but when I reflect on it, it doesn't seem long ago at
all.

However, I can remember that when I talked to my mother about
her childhood, I thought it was a long, long time ago. I often said to
her, "Back in your days," and she would say, "What do you mean

'back in my days?' I am not that old." I couldn't understand then what she meant, but now I do. Somehow, it drives the point home clearer when the shoe is on the other foot.

We also received clothes from my Aunt Cara, who lived in New York. She would often send us a box of clothes that the white folks had given her. They were real nice clothes and we were always so happy when she called to tell us a box was on the way. Some of the labels had the name, "Bobbie Robbin." I would pretend that they were designed especially for me, except that the designer had used my nickname instead of my real name.

My real father's last name was Robinson, so I pretended that the designer used my real father's name. I showed the labels to my friends and told them how my rich aunt in New York had the clothes designed especially for me; they always believed me and were very envious.

One night when the woman's husband picked me up to babysit, I was wearing a sweater with a matching skirt and a gold chain necklace. It was only gold plate, but it looked like the real thing. When we got to the house, I walked into the baby's room and while I was bending over the crib to pick the baby up, she reached for my necklace.

The little girl, who was about five years old, was standing in the room looking at me. She smiled and remarked about how pretty my necklace was. Just as she made the comment, her father walked into the room with a neighbor. When the father heard the little girl's comment he said loudly to his neighbor, "My wife has remarked about the way she (nodding his head in my direction) dresses. She wears clothes to work that are almost better than the clothes my wife wears, and if she doesn't stop wearing her jewelry to work, I may have to go out and buy my wife some new clothes and jewelry just so that she can compete with the hired help!"

When I heard this, I asked, "What does your wife suggest I wear? Something that will make me look like a fool or something that she considers appropriate for colored folks to wear?"

He answered, obviously annoyed, "I just think that she would prefer if you wouldn't try to look better than the person you work for."

I said, "O.K.," and let the conversation drop, because I had made up my mind right then and there that I didn't want to work for that woman anymore. I had noticed the little hints she made every time I came to babysit. I had also heard the remarks she made to her neighbor about the way I dressed. It wasn't that I over-dressed or tried to be sexy. She was objecting to the quality of my clothes. She must have wanted me to dress in rags or shabby clothes. That obviously was the image she had as to how "Us po cullud foks wuz posed ta dres."

The more I thought about it, the madder I got. I was so angry that I didn't want to wait until later to quit. I told the man that I had forgotten to leave the door unlocked for my younger sister and I had to go back home to open the door for her. That was a lie. Our parents did not give us keys. Whenever my sister and I were out, we had to wait until someone came home to let us into the house.

In the daytime, the key was left for us under the mat on the front porch. I said I had to go home right away and that I would return after I opened the door for my baby sister. (My baby sister was only two years younger than I and weighed about fifty pounds more.) I insisted that the father did not have to drive me home because I lived nearby and I could run home while he was dressing to go out for the evening. No, I didn't live very far away, just in another neighborhood where the pavement ended.

I put on my jacket and left the house. I knew that when I walked out of their house that night, they wouldn't have to worry about my clothes again. I walked home, seething with rage. The nerve of that woman, I thought.

When I got home, I changed into some other clothes and went to visit Janie. Mother said that the husband had been driving by our house trying to find me. He had stopped and asked Mother why I hadn't returned to babysit his children. I told Mother to tell him to find someone else his wife could tell how to dress. After that, they didn't call me again.

Frank and Mother were still fighting. One night when Mother was in the kitchen holding Al in her arms, she and Frank were arguing about another woman Mother had seen with him. I had just walked into the house when I heard Frank curse Mother and then slap her. When I saw that big, ugly ape slap my mother, I flew into a rage and hit him with my fists. I kept screaming and hitting him.

Then he turned his anger on me, and started hitting me with his fists. I ran into his and Mother's bedroom and he followed me. He backed me into a corner of the room, beating me with his fists. The punches were so severe that I thought I was going to pass out. The only thing I could reach was a can opener on the dresser. I grabbed it, lashed out, and kept swinging. I cut Frank on his chest and when he saw his blood he got scared and said I was crazy and trying to kill him. I told him that if he ever hit my mother again, I would kill him and I'd smile all the way to the gas chamber. He was such a bully.

As long as he was intimidating me he was fine, but as soon as he saw me fighting back without fear of being hurt or even killed, he was afraid of what I might do to him. He called the police and told them I had tried to kill him. "After all I did for her," he said to the policeman who responded to his call. Frank told me to get out of his house. The policeman told me that I should be ashamed for fighting with my father. It didn't seem to matter that I was protecting my mother. The policeman went on scolding me and telling me how I should be grateful and how good I had it, not like the Carpenters who didn't live as well as we did.

The Carpenters were a black family who lived about four blocks from us on a small street and were considered to be the poorest family in East Wynnton. They had a lot of very bad children, mostly boys, who were always in trouble with the police. Every weekend it seemed that someone in the family was arrested. None of the children had finished school.

As a matter of fact, two of the boys who were in my class had dropped out of school. They lived in a house that didn't have electric- ity, but they stuck together. If you hit one, you had to fight the whole family, so nobody bothered them. Sometimes we thought the police harassed them because they were poor and colored. At least they didn't have to worry about a father who beat on them all the time.

So this good, white policeman was standing there telling me how thankful I should be because of the type of house in which I lived. It didn't matter that we were being abused. It didn't matter that I was standing there with a swollen lip, my eye almost closed, and blood all over me; I just should have been thankful. But I wasn't. I packed my clothes in brown paper bags that night and I left Frank's house. I never returned.

Do Kin Folks Care?

After I had cut Frank for beating my mother, I went to live with my Aunt Maelizzie. She was Mother's oldest sister who couldn't stand Mother's drinking.

Life with Maelizzie was very difficult and very trying, to say the least. Maelizzie didn't have children of her own and she had been mean to me when I was growing up. She would do whatever she could to help me if I really needed it, but she would never let me forget it either.

She had been married to Bob for as long as I could remember. Bob worked for the railroad all of his life, yet he had never learned to read, write, or drive a car. It always amazed me that Bob went everywhere on foot. I often saw him walking past the high school I attended. He had a thing about taxicabs. He didn't trust cab drivers, and he wouldn't ride in cars or buses. He said he didn't trust any of them; he trusted his own legs more. Bob always wore bib overalls, a railroad cap, and a red railroad kerchief.

I tried to adjust to living with Maelizzie and Bob until graduation that June. I wanted to graduate from high school more than anything.

I couldn't forget the promise I had made myself to finish school and I couldn't forget the promise I had made when Mama died.

I knew I could no longer live with Mother and Frank, which meant that either Maelizzie and Bob or prostitution. I could have gotten married, but I wasn't ready for that type of commitment. I could have made a lot of money being a prostitute. I was an attractive young lady and I lived in an army town where men were plentiful and willing to buy. The soldiers would have paid handsomely for my body, I was told.

But I wasn't that kind of girl; I wanted more than that from life and I figured education was the only way to get it. I knew the only way that a colored woman could battle the white man's system and win was by using her mind, not her body. Still, I found odd jobs for extra money. Mother was drinking very heavily every day and I was feeling sorry for myself.

Christmas came while I was living with Maelizzie and Bob. I felt especially sad, because I wanted to be with my family during the holidays. I took all the money I had saved and bought everyone in my family a Christmas present, even Frank. On Christmas Day, I rode the bus to visit Mother, bringing my presents. When I walked onto the front porch I was glad to see how beautifully the house was decorated and how pretty the Christmas tree looked through the big picture window. However, I felt as if I were a stranger in a house I had once called home.

I felt as if I were visiting acquaintances, not friends, just acquaintances. I was once part of this family, I thought as I looked through the window at the decorated tree with all the fancy wrapped presents under it and the fire burning in the fireplace. Christmas carols were playing on the radio and I could smell Mother's sweet potato and apple pies baking in the oven. I knew she had already finished her chocolate cake and was waiting for it to cool before putting on the chocolate icing and decorating it with freshly shelled pecans. I knew her Christmas ritual. I had enjoyed it for so many years, and now I was on the outside looking in.

I began to feel as if I were standing on someone else's porch, about to knock on a stranger's door. I paused and thought, "How strange this all feels now. I really don't have a place to call home. There is no room for me anywhere." Tears began to well up in my eyes but I refused to cry. Hurriedly, I wiped my eyes, put a big smile on my face, and knocked on the door.

Mother came to the door and welcomed me with a hug and a "Merry Christmas" greeting. I hugged her back and walked into the front room and began looking at what everyone had gotten for Christmas.

Sandy happily showed me her new Scotch plaid car coat and matching pants, and lots of skirts and sweaters. Al had gotten a red wagon, trucks, clothes, and a lot of other toys. He pulled on my arm, eager to show me what Santa Claus had brought him, "Cause I had been a good boy, Bobba," he gleefully told me, trying to pronounce my name.

Frank had bought Mother a new suit, shoes, a cashmere coat, a beautiful housecoat with matching house shoes and other personal items. Everyone had bought Frank presents like house shoes, shirts, pajamas, sweaters, and lots of other things. There was candy, fruits, and nuts under the tree. I gave everyone the presents I had bought for them and watched them smile as they opened the boxes, delighted in discovering what was inside. But there wasn't anything for me, not even a Christmas card. I was so hurt that no one thought enough of me to buy me at least a pair of socks.

I tried not to show my hurt and disappointment and struggled hard to fight back the tears. I kept telling myself that it didn't matter and that one day I would be with people who really loved me and I would look back on all of this and laugh. I told myself that they had meant to buy me something but they had forgotten and that I would get something later. I told myself all those things, but I didn't believe them.

I loved my mother, sister, and brother, and I missed not being with them every day. I especially missed not waking up with them on Christmas Day as I had done for so many years, smelling Mother's cake and pies mixed with the smells of fruit and nuts and the pine scent of the Christmas tree.

Maelizzie and Bob had not given me anything either, although I had given them Christmas presents. Actually, they didn't even celebrate Christmas. They had not even decorated their house for the season.

I sat there admiring their presents and listening to them thanking each other. When I felt that I could no longer hold back my tears, I kissed everyone good-bye, wished them a Merry Christmas, and left. I cried all the way to the bus stop. Mother didn't even ask me to stay for dinner, and strangely, now that I think about it, no one asked me what I got for Christmas. I was crying so hard that a woman stopped and asked me if I was sick. That was the last Christmas I spent at home, if you could call that home.

Janie and I frequently worked as waitresses at the Officers' Club in Fort Benning, Georgia. The officers reserved the club for parties on special occasions such as retirements, weddings, anniversaries, or graduations. On those occasions the club employed additional serving help for the event. There were other times when an officer, such as a major or a general, would have a party at his home and it would be catered by the Officers' Club. On those occasions also, the club would hire additional help. Those were the times when Janie and I worked as waitresses for the club.

In addition to the main club, there were several smaller clubs scattered throughout the base. When an affair was scheduled for one of the smaller clubs, the main club hired additional help, such as waiters, busboys, waitresses, and bartenders. The additional help were transported to those locations in vans and returned to the main club when the affair was over.

Although we earned a decent income as waitresses, we could have earned much more if we were different types of girls. Every time we worked a party, regardless of location, there would be some officer who would proposition us. It didn't matter what race they were. They seemed to prefer "cullud girls."

Sometimes they would pay one of the waiters or busboys to give us messages and would promise to pay them more should they persuade us to go out with them. One officer, giving the party at his home, offered to leave his wife and guests and go with us that night. They were wild about good-looking black women, especially the older white officers. Janie and I had other ideas about the quality of our lives. Neither of us had been involved sexually with men. We used our earnings to buy clothes and other things that our parents couldn't afford.

Sometimes we sat and talked about how much money we could make if we prostituted our bodies. We often questioned if we were foolish because we really did need the money, and, after all, who would know? The answer was that we would know. It didn't matter what other people thought about us. We were our own best friends and we couldn't have self-respect if we did what we knew to be wrong. Janie and I were both brought up in the church. We both had a strong Christian faith. I was a Baptist and Janie was a Sanctified Holy. Members did the "Holy Dance" at Janie's church when they were filled with the Holy Ghost.

It may have been our belief in God that gave us the strong self-esteem that kept us from becoming prostitutes. We both had so many family problems, but we loved self-respect more than we did money. Despite its shortcomings, I loved working at the Officers' Club. The atmosphere was luxurious. There were not many black officers who attended or used the club facilities. Janie and I pretended that we were there as guests, not as servants. But we promised ourselves that we would return as guests some day and we would be treated in the same grand style that we used when serving others. We made good our promise.

I loved shrimp cocktails and I especially loved the cocktail sauce the club's chef made. Every meal began with shrimp cocktails. There were always a few shrimp missing from the tables that I served. I took as many as I could before their absence would be detected.

One day the Executive Director of the club called me into his office. He told me that I was in danger of going to jail because I had been forging false social security numbers on my pay vouchers. I didn't know what he was talking about. He asked me what my social security number was. I told him that I didn't have a social security number.

Then he asked me how I had been filling in social security numbers when I got my paycheck. I said that I just made them up and wrote them in. I never used the same numbers again because I couldn't remember them. I just made up a new number every time I needed one. I didn't know that I was doing something illegal.

I knew that each time you earned money the government would take some of it out of your earnings and apply it to the social security number you used. Then, in your old age, the amount of money the government had deposited under your specific number would be the amount of money you could receive from the Social Security Administration. Therefore, because I was inventing numbers, and I figured that they probably belonged to others, it meant that the government was applying the money they had deducted from my earnings to the accounts of the various numbers I had invented. I remember thinking, "I guess when some people get old, they are going to wonder where all that social security money was coming from." It was as if I were a mysterious giver. Boy, oh, boy!! Now when I think about it, how dumb could I have been?

When the Director asked me what I thought would happen to me when I used phony social security numbers, I answered, "I told you, I just thought that someone else would receive the benefits." He explained to me the seriousness of incorrect use of social security numbers. I immediately got myself a social security card.

Chocolate cake was, and still is, my favorite cake. Before we began working, it was customary for the extra help to go into the mess hall, prepare our trays, and take them into the dining hall designated for the employees, and eat our dinner there before we began work. The employees' dining hall had long wooden benches and tables. This was done so that we wouldn't eat the food that had been prepared for the guests.

One night, when I was preparing my plate, I noticed the baker was baking a lot of chocolate cake for a party. Later, every chance I had I slipped into the bakery and stole a piece of cake. We were allowed a twenty-minute break, so when my break came, I went back into the bakery and there wasn't anyone there. There was, however, a large chocolate sheet cake on the counter.

I took the entire cake and hid in a corner of the bakery where I couldn't be seen, and proceeded to eat the entire cake. I don't know how long I had been in the corner eating cake because I forgot about the time. As I sat there, I looked up and saw the Director leaning over the counter looking at me. I was eating the cake with my hands because I didn't have access to eating utensils.

I jumped when I saw him. I must have been a funny sight to see, hiding in the corner with chocolate all around my mouth and all over my hands and my clothes where I had wiped my hands. "That's all right," he said. "Enjoy yourself, because when you finish eating cake, you're fired."

I had seen him use that tactic on Steve, one of the boys who often worked with us. Steve was working two jobs and going to school; therefore, he was often very tired. He sometimes hid in the men's locker room for a quick nap, and we all covered for him, because he was such a likeable guy.

One night when Steve had been off the floor for an unusually long period of time, the Director went looking for him. He walked into the food pantry and opened the door to find Steve lying on the floor in a corner asleep and snoring very loudly. Philip, another helper, started to wake Steve, but the Director stopped him saying, "That's all right. Let him sleep. As long as he is asleep, he has a job, but as soon as he wakes up, he's fired."

So, I knew he was true to his word, and, because I was fired anyway, I just sat there and finished the cake. Then I got sick and went home.

I felt that it was just a matter of time before he fired Janie and me anyway because of another incident. The previous week we had been sent to work a party at one of the smaller clubs. The manager of that club was an older white man who loved young colored girls. He told Janie and me to take off our clothes, including our underpanties and put on short white jackets he gave us. The jackets were those that waiters and busboys wore when serving parties.

All the females were required to wear white uniform dresses, which were always made available to us. We would arrive at the main club in our street clothes and go into a designated dressing area where there were lockers and showers. There was a specified area for males and another for females. However, because this club was so far away from the main club, the additional help were required to go directly to the smaller club and change into the uniforms that were to be provided there. But that night, there weren't any dresses, only jackets.

After the manager tried to make Janie and me wear the short jackets, he told us that he intended to have us work the pantry instead of serving the guests. In the pantry, we would be required to go up and down step ladders to get whatever he told us to get. This we were to do without benefit of underpanties.

Janie and I both cursed him out and walked to the bus stop, which was approximately ten miles through a lonely stretch of dirt country woods. We were both scared to death to be walking alone, but we couldn't stay at the club because the manager told us to leave if we refused to follow his instructions, and we refused. He wouldn't allow us to wait at the club for transportation, which was the van that carried employees to and from the bus stop.

Janie and I reported the incident to the Director at the main club, but the manager had already called him, lying that Janie and I were lousy workers and that the work was different there than at the main club, and as a result we had refused to do as instructed. Furthermore, Janie and I, he claimed, had tried to seduce one of the supervisors; therefore, it was necessary to fire us. He went on to say that he had suggested that we wait for the van to return so that we could ride safely to the bus stop, but we had met some soldiers and we left with them in a car.

When we told the Director that the manager was lying, naturally, because we were nothing but colored teenagers, our word against that of a white man, especially a manager, was not believed.

Then my worry was how to get the money to pay for my senior expenses. Maelizzie made it clear that the only thing she could provide so that I could graduate in June was a place to sleep. She made it perfectly clear that she and Bob didn't have children and that they could not afford to take care of somebody else's child. I still had to take care of myself financially. Every time Maelizzie cooked, I got the feeling that she didn't want me to eat her food. She made me feel that she only cooked enough for Bob and herself.

One day when I came home after studying at the library, there wasn't any food left for me. Maelizzie and Bob had eaten their dinner, but they didn't leave anything for me. I had saved a little money from working at the club. The money was for bus fare to and from school and for lunch money. I was just about to walk out the door to go buy something to eat when the telephone rang. It was the police informing us that they had just arrested Mother for drunk and disorderly conduct. Maelizzie began calling Mother names and said that for all she cared Mother could just keep her "drunken ass in jail until she rots."

I was not about to let my mother stay in jail. I took the money I had saved, called a taxi, went to the jail, and bailed out my mother. She walked out with her clothes in disarray; she was wearing just one boot, although it was winter. I couldn't stand to see her like that, so I paid the cab driver to take her home. I didn't ride home with her, remembering that every time she was drunk she wanted to beat and curse me.

I took another cab back toward Maelizzie's house, as far as my money would permit me to ride. When we were about ten blocks from Maelizzie's, I realized I didn't have enough money to pay for the entire distance. I told the cabbie to let me out, and I walked the rest of the way.

When I arrived I was tired, hungry, and very depressed, but I wouldn't let Maelizzie see me cry. Although I cried every step of the way back, as soon as I turned into Maelizzie's yard, I wiped the tears from my eyes. I walked into the house and said as cheerfully as I could, "Mother is all right. She was glad to see me."

I tried to make Mother's incarceration sound like a joke, but it didn't come out that way. My voice was trembling and I walked out of the room before the tears started to roll down my cheeks. Maelizzie must have felt sorry for me because she came into the front room where I was sitting in the dark and gave me a quarter to go across the street to buy two hot dogs for dinner (they were two-for-a-quarter at the store across the street). I cried myself to sleep that night and prayed that I could just bear the pressure and make it until graduation in June. After that night, I began to concentrate completely on my senior oration. I wanted mine to be so outstanding that years after my graduation, the teachers would still talk about the lasting impression I had made on the student body.

Preparing to write and present a memorable oration meant spending a lot of time in the library; it meant spending a lot of my days and nights writing and researching my material; it meant that many times I didn't go to lunch, because I spent my lunch hours either with my senior advisor or with my homeroom teacher getting advice and instructions on how to prepare my oration. However, I was determined that, regardless of the price, if not the best, I was going to be one of the best. I wanted Mother to be proud of me, and I wanted every other parent who would attend the senior oration program on the day I was to give mine to envy my mother, because her daughter was the best.

The day finally arrived for my group to give our senior orations. I was so proud when I peeked from behind the curtains backstage and saw Mother sitting in the front row of the auditorium looking as sharp as a tack. She was really looking good. I thought that she was the best-looking person in the audience. I knew that every man in there had noticed her. Plus, she had not had anything to drink.

Mrs. Hunt, the seventh grade teacher who had told me so many years ago that I wouldn't graduate from school and that she doubted I would make it to the ninth grade, was sitting in the front row. I had made a point of sending her an invitation to come as one of my special guests to hear my senior oration. I felt I had to prove a point to her which was: "Regardless of what type of family I come from, who and what I become is my own responsibility."

There were six of us speaking that day. The stage was decorated with beautiful flowers that we had purchased from a local florist. We had also gotten corsages for our parents and we pinned them on our mothers before the program began.

The title of my oration was, *The Sun Never Sets, It Just Goes*

Down. It was about the plight of the Negro people from slavery to freedom. I used Langston Hughes's book, *The Negro Caravan,* as my main reference book.

I was always fascinated by the strength of the black race during slavery. It always fascinated me how a people could be so oppressed and depressed, yet endure and emerge always singing, always with hope, and always praising God for His goodness. That was the most fascinating part - we were always singing and talking about a better place "when we gits home."

In my oration, I talked about the slave whose eyes saw, "Chariots swing low," the slave whose ears heard "Great Jordan Roll," and the slave who breathed that sweet melodic cry, "Nobody knows de trouble I seen." I talked about the Negro washwoman, the strong black woman, the tall yellow woman, and the gentle brown woman. I talked about the black race as being God's flowerbed of people with every color of man being in the black race, from the blackest Black to the person who may be indistinguishable from the white race, and all the shades in between.

I talked about how families were torn apart as they were sold on the auction blocks. I talked about how the Negro mothers would beg slave owners with anguished cries, "Please massah, buy my chillun."

I talked about how our slave ancestors found a tree and used it as a church, a place to worship, because that was all they had. I talked about how the white plantation owners would kill a pig, eat the best parts and give the intestines, the head, the ears, the feet, and all the insides of the pig to the slaves. Yet the slaves turned that stuff into meals that are traditional today. I guess that is why we are a people who have so much respect, get so involved with, and depend so much on, our religious beliefs. There was a time in slavery when that was all we had.

I began my speech saying, "Light, light, give me light. Let me see that sweet light of freedom before I die." That was the cry that was heard as families were being torn apart and auctioned off separately in the slave markets. I spoke of the sound of slaves crying and begging the slave owners "Please buy my chillun, Massah. Dey don't eat much and dey strong. Please Massah, buy my chillun." I ended saying, "The sun never sets. It just goes down, only to rise again."

One of Langston Hughes's poems is about a Negro washwoman. It talks about a, "Tall yellow woman…a strong black woman…clothes washed clean, soul washed clean, for you I have many songs to sing, if I could but find the words." It reminded me of my grandmother, because she was a washwoman. That was one of the reasons I used the poem in my speech.

The white folks brought their dirty clothes to Mama's house in large bags and she boiled them in her old, black, washpot in the backyard. She then soaked them in her homemade soap and scrubbed them on the scrub board in the tin tubs until her knuckles were raw. The water had to be drawn from the well. When the clothes were white and clean, she hung them on lines that were strung from the house to the chicken fence in the backyard, and let them hang in the bright sunshine until they were dry. Then she took them into the house and ironed them using irons that she heated on the stove - she couldn't afford an electric iron.

Mama had two "flat irons." One sat heating on the stove while she used the other. She starched the collars of men's shirts and the white women's dresses so stiff they could almost stand up by themselves. When she ironed the clothes, there wasn't a wrinkle to be found on them. Mama bought starch that came as white lumps in a box. She boiled the lumps in water to make a paste and then strained it through a piece of cloth. The white folks loved to have Mama take care of their clothes. They only paid her $1.25 per load, and they were big loads.

The audience loved it! The teachers, my mother and some of the guests were crying when I finished. A hush had fallen over the audience while I was speaking. Afterwards, some of my classmates said to me, "Girl, you had that audience eating out of the palm of your hands. We didn't know you could speak like that." Boy, was I proud of myself! And what made it so much better was the fact that Mrs. Hunt was sitting on the front row crying with the other guests. Yes, that was truly MY DAY!

After my oration and after witnessing my acting ability in our senior play, my teachers began to notice that I had certain abilities that previously had not been recognized. Because self-confidence was not stressed at home, I tended to be shy. Furthermore, I was often ridiculed by my peers. My teachers didn't know that I had such a clear speaking voice, yet I had been in their classes for years.

But then again, I wasn't light skinned with long hair either, and my mother was not a teacher. That was the black race's way of discriminating against each other.

We had been so indoctrinated to the white man's way of thinking and the white man's perception of beauty, that we didn't like ourselves. We wanted to get as near to white as we could, by preferring light complexioned partners, using bleaching cream on our skin, straightening our hair with a straightening comb, burning our scalps using chemicals on our hair to make it straight, and not wearing light colors because we were told that dark-skinned people should not wear "loud colors."

I think that almost every Negro woman who lived in the South and had dark skin must have worn Red Fox stockings, used Nut Brown face powder and raspberry lipstick - I wonder if they still make those? My teachers asked me why I hadn't let anyone know about my speaking, acting, and writing abilities until it was almost time for me to graduate. I told them that basically I was shy and didn't talk much. They knew that was a lie. My eighth grade teacher at Carver Heights School, Mrs. Pendleton, wrote on the back of one of my school pictures, "A very smart young lady, but she can talk a hungry dog off a meat wagon." Every teacher I had told me how much I talked.

I think the reason that I didn't let anyone know about my talents was because I feared rejection. Yet, I had written a play while I was in the fifth grade, and another when I was in the eighth. I was to portray one of the characters in the play that I had written when I was in the eighth grade. It was for a school talent show, which was to be presented in the school auditorium for the parents and the entire student body. However, because the program was too long, some of the performances had to be eliminated and one of those cut was the comedy I had written.

I was very disappointed and took the cut as a rejection and I never bothered to write again, nor did I bother to try acting until I won one of the lead roles in our senior play.

I didn't have as much confidence in myself as I pretended. I always put on a front and pretended things didn't bother me and that the kids teasing me about my mother and father didn't hurt me, but none of that was true. It did hurt me and I did care. I think that if my parents had been different or even if my mother hadn't been an alcoholic in a small town where everybody knew us, and if she had taken more interest in our schooling, Sandy and I would have been involved in more school activities.

Sandy had a beautiful singing voice, and she had a talent for sewing. Frank had a beautiful singing voice and he could play a heck of a saxophone. In fact, he owned one, but he pawned it once and never went to redeem it. He always sang in some of the local clubs. If we had cultivated our talents, man, think of where we could have gone with them! Maybe it was not Mother's fault. If we really tried, we could have been famous. I don't want to blame Mother; she is not here to defend herself now, and besides, she was ill with the disease of alcoholism.

After the day's orations were finished, I introduced Mother to my teachers and friends. Then I said to Mother, "Remember when you came to school to pick me up in Daddy's car?" I didn't mention that she had been drinking that day. I saw no need to hurt her by rehashing bad experiences. She knew what I was talking about when I mentioned "coming to school in Daddy's car."

She smiled and said, "Yes, I remember very well. I wish I could forget it and I hope that you have forgiven me." She didn't have to ask me to forgive her. I loved her, of course I forgave her. I always did.

I said, "Well, the lady who was sitting next to you in the auditorium when I was giving my oration was the lady whose car you hit that day, and the girl who was sitting next to me on stage and gave her oration before I gave mine is her daughter."

We both began to laugh and couldn't stop. I suspect that we were each thinking the same thing - that Mother had promised to pay for the damages to the lady's car. Mother really didn't think that they would see each other again. Yet, by coincidence, here they were both together, both of their daughters speaking on the same day, with honors.

By the time I gave my senior oration, Frank had been jailed by the army. Mother told us that Frank had hit an officer in the mouth because the officer called him a "nigga." Years later Sandy and I learned that Frank actually had been locked up for forgery. He had gone to a downtown finance company with a woman who was impersonating Mother. There, they took out a loan against our house. The woman signed Mother's name on the papers. We would also learn that Frank had fathered the woman's baby. It was a boy about the same age as my brother Al.

We lost the house when Frank was sent to jail and Mother couldn't make the loan payments. She went to the welfare agency for help and they refused. The white folks tried to make her take me out of school and put me to work to help pay the loan and other bills that she and Frank had incurred, but she refused. The white man said to her, "Take that biggun outta school and put her to work. Ain't got no need fer edjucation no how. Needs to be hepin' wid dese bills. Hi-fer-loot'n Nigras."

Mother asked the white man, "Suppose you owed me money. Would you take your child out of school and make her go to work in order to pay me?"

The white man replied, "Hell Naw."

Mother told him, "That's the same damn way I feel about what I owe you. My children will not suffer for my mistakes. To hell with you and your system. I will pay you what I can, when I can, and if that ain't good enough for you, put me in jail and you won't get a damn penny, plus you'll be taking care of that 'biggun' and that 'litteun' too."

The man was so angry with Mother that he turned red in the face. He was chewing tobacco and the spittle was in the corner of his mouth, plus he had yellow teeth. He wasn't half as clean as Mother; his shirt collar was dirty, and he smelled like old sweat. Furthermore, he couldn't speak as well as Mother, yet he was a caseworker. He denied Mother any benefits. He would not approve any assistance for us because he insisted that Mother take me out of school. But that feisty lady stood her ground and was just as adamant as he.

Mother went to another social service department to try to get assistance. They also wanted her to take me out of school and put me to work to help repay the debts. That was the way the white folks in the South kept black people from progressing; stacking the cards against them so that their children were forced to quit school and go to work to help with the bills.

When the man at the last place Mother went for assistance told her to take me out of school, she told him where he could go, what he could do when he got there, and who he could take with him. He turned as red as a beet. I laughed so hard. Mother was furious with the system. She was something else when it came to our education. She always told us to, "Get a good education first, because that is the best foundation any colored person can get, and that is the one thing that the white folks cannot take from you."

Mother would wake up at night cursing the white folks in her sleep. She said she was dreaming about them harassing her for money that she didn't have. She often said that she could hear them calling her name in her sleep, in that slow, southern drawl that would get on her nerves. They didn't want to accept payments. They wanted all the money at once, or at least larger payments than she was able to make.

I admired her for standing up to them, even though she stood alone. She never admitted it, but she was very depressed because she had lost the only house she had ever owned, and come to think of it, she never owned another. Not only had she lost the house, she also lost all her furniture.

I could never understand why she stayed with Frank after he put her through that kind of humiliation; getting another woman to impersonate her and forge her signature; losing everything she owned; and to top it all off, having an affair with the woman and having a child by her. Lord, my mother was a beautiful woman inside and out. Her only crime was alcoholism and that was an illness. How I wish I could have helped her. I could never understand her loyalty to Frank.

I lived with Maelizzie and Bob until the finance company foreclosed on the house and took it from Mother. Mother, Sandy, and Al were still living in the house at the time. It was just five months before graduation and I was trying desperately to hold on for those five months. After Mother lost the house, she, Al, and Sandy moved into a one bedroom apartment. They were called apartments, but they looked more like projects to me, because they all had the same kind of fixtures, cement walls, and concrete floors.

When we walked into the kitchen and turned on the light, the counter top was covered with roaches. On the other hand, at least there was a bathtub and bathroom located inside the house, so we no longer had to go outside to use the toilet. Even at Maelizzie's house the toilet was out in the backyard, and we had to share it with the next door neighbor; there was no sink, just the commode. But, in the new apartment, we had a sink in the bathroom with hot and cold running water. There was also a sink in the kitchen with hot and cold running water. I left Maelizzie's and Bob's house and moved back with Mother to try to help her pay expenses.

All four of us slept in the one tiny bedroom. Mother and I were the only two family members who were working. I could always find a job somewhere, even if it was only babysitting.

Sandy babysat with little Al while Mother and I worked. I had found a job as a counter girl with the local USO. It seemed that I always found jobs where there were lots of soldiers; perhaps that is why people couldn't believe that I was still a virgin. Even Mother didn't believe it.

Mother had bought Sandy a used sewing machine for her birthday, but we needed money for food and the rent. Mother told me not to go to school one day; she needed me to stay at home and help her take care of some business. While Sandy was at school, Mother and I loaded the sewing machine into the old 98 Oldsmobile (that the finance company later repossessed), and took the sewing machine to a pawn shop where we hocked it to get money for food and rent. After three months in the apartment, it was apparent that Mother couldn't make enough money to meet expenses, even with my help, which wasn't much.

She refused to take me out of school, yet she knew she would have to move in with Maelizzie and Bob, because there wasn't anywhere else to go. I knew she would hate to do that. When the finance company finally took the car and what little furniture was left, she had no other choice but to go to live with Maelizzie and Bob. Maelizzie said that she didn't have enough room for all of us so, Mother, Sandy and Al moved in with Maelizzie and Bob. Mother, Sandy and Al were sleeping in the front room on Maelizzie's sofa, which opened out into a bed.

I felt sorry for them, because I knew their lives were miserable.

I was left again to fend for myself. I was just seventeen, but I felt as if I had lived a long, hard lifetime. I had no idea where I was going to live. I just wanted to graduate from school. That was the only thing I could think about. I knew that I couldn't afford an apartment, pay for school expenses and other living expenses, and buy food with my pay from working part time at the USO Club.

Janie had an aunt who lived across the street from the apartment where we had lived. She told her aunt that I didn't have anywhere to go. She rented me a room and, Lord, did my troubles compound themselves.

Hard Knocks, But My Way

Janie's aunt was called "Dear." I never did know her real name. Dear ran a boarding and rooming house for soldiers and their families. I agreed to pay her seven dollars every two weeks for a room.

There were three families living in Dear's rooming house. She really didn't have enough space in her house for me, but because I was a friend of Janie's, she made room. There was a tiny dining room that separated the kitchen from the living room. Dear moved a little cot into that room and that was where I slept. The room was so tiny that only a dresser could fit in it.

To make matters worse, all the other rooms had doors that opened into my tiny room, except for one bedroom off the back porch that was occupied by a young soldier and his family. I kept my clothes and the few personal things that I constantly used in boxes under my cot. Other clothes and various articles were packed in boxes and stored in a closet on Dear's back porch. Unfortunately, there was only one telephone in the house and it was located in my little room, right next to my cot.

As a matter of fact, in order to use the telephone it was necessary to either sit on my cot or to reach across it. Also, the only access to the one bathroom or to the living room was through the small dining room. This meant that there was always a lot of traffic through the area where I slept.

A young soldier and his wife were living in the rooming house. They had one child, but the husband was not the father. His wife had the child before she met him. The soldier beat the little boy all the time for any little thing. Sometimes he just slapped the three-year-old across the mouth just for asking questions.

Once we heard the wife screaming. When we rushed into the back room we found that the soldier had tied her hands and feet to the bed and was beating her with a stick while the woman's little boy was made to stand and watch. This made me feel sick, because I knew of all the times the soldier had come into my room to talk on the phone with other women and I had heard him tell them how much he hated his wife and "bastard" child.

The soldier was friendly with another soldier in the house named Johnny, and I thought that Johnny was one of the ugliest men I had ever seen but his wife was the nicest person.

One night when I worked at the USO, the young soldier and Johnny both were at a dance there. The USO sponsored a dance every Saturday night. There were always a lot of soldiers there and a lot of my girlfriends and schoolmates attended, but Janie and I never did. The dances were held in the second floor dance hall and I worked on the main floor in the recreation area where the snack shop was.

When Johnny and the other soldier learned I was working there, they kept coming downstairs and ordering food. They insisted on taking me home after the club closed, but I refused. Johnny had been drinking and the more he drank the uglier he got, and the uglier he got the more he wanted to get close to me. He kept looking at me in a strange way that frightened me. When they finally accepted that I was not going to ride home with them, they left. Later I took a cab home.

The manager of the USO always walked me to the cab to make sure I was safe, because sometimes the soldiers got wild after they had been drinking. Although the USO didn't sell alcohol and no one was allowed to take alcoholic beverages upstairs to the dance, they still managed to get it into the building and into their stomachs.

I was in bed later that night and I felt the cover being removed from my body. God must have awakened me, because I am usually a very sound sleeper. I turned over and saw, standing beside my bed, the ugly soldier, Johnny, with food and alcohol on his breath. He was nude and had an erection. He was holding his penis in one hand and grinning at me with that strange look on his ugly face that had frightened me earlier.

I looked up at him and said, "If you don't get your ugly ass away from me I will call your wife." At first he wouldn't leave. He kept telling me how beautiful I was and how much he wanted to make love to me. He kept saying how he had dreamed of me every night since he first saw me and how he could think of nothing else but me. He kept telling me about how he wanted to take care of me.

By then his other hand was under the cover searching for my body. There was a full moon and my bed was directly under the window. There were curtains at the window, but there was no shade on it. Johnny looked grotesque standing there naked in the moonlight with his ugly self, his flat behind, his pot belly, and a hard-on. If I hadn't been so scared, I would have laughed at the sight of him. But I couldn't let on that I was afraid.

I tried to sound brave as I threatened him. While he was bending over reaching for me under the bed covers, I kicked him in the groin as hard as I could, then I said in a menacing voice that masked my fear, "Go ahead and holler you bastard, and everyone in this house will be out here including your wife."

He must have been really hurting because I kicked him with every ounce of strength I had. He grabbed his penis with one hand and covered his mouth with the other, trying to stifle his screams of pain.

I didn't call out for help because I was afraid that Dear would put me out, and claim that I started trouble and had encouraged his attentions. After all, he had been living there before me, and he was obviously paying Dear more rent and board than I was. Actually, I wasn't paying board. I ate wherever and whenever I could.

I stayed awake all that night. I was too scared to sleep. The next morning I told Dear what had happened. I hoped that if I told her, she would protect me by at least keeping an eye on Johnny, especially when he had been drinking. I didn't want any trouble with his wife, that was why I thought it better to tell Dear about it. After all, I was her niece's best friend and Dear had known me all my life.

But, instead of protecting me, she accused me of enticing him. She said that he was a paying resident and if anyone was going to leave, it would be me because girls like me were only trouble. Girls like me? That remark really hurt. Why would I be living that way if I was the kind of girl she thought I was?

I really couldn't understand why Dear thought of me the way she did. I bought my own food, cooked my own meals whenever I ate there, which wasn't often, washed my own clothes, had a job, not much, but a job so I could at least pay my own way.

Dear was very fair-skinned and had wavy hair. Janie's entire family was just the opposite of my family; my family was very dark-complexioned. Dear was not at all attractive. She smoked too much, had little, straight legs, and walked very fast, almost running, as if she was always in a hurry. She was the type of person who never had anything good to say about anyone. Yet, she had a way of making you think that she was your friend and that you could trust her.

Dear's husband was just as dark as Dear was light. His name was George and we called him "Uncle George." Uncle George was a very heavy-set, short, stocky man who walked with a limp, and he was always cursing Dear. He drove a big, black car that he kept parked in the backyard. Dear couldn't drive, so Uncle George drove her everywhere.

Dear seemed to want me to stay with her and she said she admired my determination to go to college in spite of all the odds against me. She gave me the impression that she would provide the home stability that a young teen-aged girl needed. Boy, was I wrong! I had explained to her that I only wanted to live with her temporarily, just until school was over in June, which was only about two months away, and then I would leave for college.

I still didn't know how I was going to college. I knew if there was a way to go, I would find it, and when I did, that would make me proud, rather than ashamed of the person who would gaze back at me from the mirror in the morning. My life's ambition was to go to college and I thought that Dear sincerely wanted to help me. I thought that was why she charged me so little to live in her house.

After I had lived with her for about two weeks, I realized that she had accepted me as a roomer for such low rent because she thought that I would be so grateful for a place to stay that I would do her household chores; in other words, become her maid. I learned from one of my friends that Dear had told her mother and some other neighbors that my own family did not want me and if I could keep her house clean and her boarders happy, it was well worth the mere three dollars and fifty cents a week I was paying her. She thought that she had snagged a live-in maid and that I would do whatever she told me to just to have a place to stay.

I didn't have time to do Dear's housework. I was still going to school during the day and working at the USO at night. I was always so tired, but I still had to study. On my days off I visited my family and cleaned my clothes. I didn't know anything about living alone and taking care of myself, but I sure learned in an hurry.

After Dear realized that I wasn't going to be her maid, she began to discuss the situation with her friends. One day she asked me into her room for a talk, and she said, "Since you are not happy living here and I am not happy with you living here, I have talked to a friend of mine who also rents rooms. She has agreed to let you stay there until school is out, and she will only charge you a dollar more than what I am charging you if you will do her house cleaning."

I began to sweat. I didn't know the woman about whom she was talking, nor was I familiar with the section of town where the woman lived. I was being tossed out again. I asked Dear if I could think about it and let her know my answer the following day. She agreed, but she said it had to be the following day for certain because the lady was anxious to rent the vacant room.

At that time I had started dating an army lieutenant, Gene, who was stationed at Fort Benning Georgia. Gene's home was in Norfolk, Virginia and he had graduated from Virginia State University. I was very glad that Gene was in my life. I don't know what I would have done without his moral support. I asked Gene to come and get me because I needed to talk. When he arrived, Dear was at home and she answered the door.

She was all sweetness and smiles for Gene, giving no hint of our recent conversation. Gene was good looking, tall, slim, and brown-skinned. During our conversation of the previous day, Dear had said, "Perhaps your soldier boyfriend can give you some money to move somewhere else. He might want you to move to a place where he can spend the night with you." Because she was all sweetness and smiles that day, she must have known that I would tell him what she had said.

Gene and I drove to the Five-O-One Drive-In, parked, and ordered sodas. I sat there and began to cry. Gene just let me cry until I felt better. Then he asked me if I was ready to talk about it. I told him what Dear had said. He sat and listened without speaking until I had finished.

I told him about Jeff, the man who owned the Five-O-One Drive-In and how he had been after me to be his girlfriend for a long time. I recalled the time when Gene and I were sitting in a nightclub next door to the Liberty Theater, which was the only all-black movie theater in Columbus. The waitress told me that I had a telephone call in the owner's private office. She said it was a very important call.

I didn't know the owner, and I had never been in the nightclub before. The boys I knew in high school couldn't afford a place like that. Also, the nightclub was one of Frank's hangouts, and if he ever caught me there, he would beat me. However, Frank was locked up then and I was on my own.

I knew that Frank knew the owner of the nightclub, Carl Greentree. I thought perhaps it was Mr. Greentree calling to tell me that something had happened to my mother, or that I was too young to be in there and I would have to leave.

However, when I answered the phone I was surprised to hear Jeff Martin's voice, the owner of the Five-O-One Drive-In. The call was not on Mr. Greentree's private line, as the waitress had said. Instead, Jeff was in another part of the nightclub talking to me on the private intercom system, and he had paid the waitress to lie for him. Jeff told me that I should get rid of my escort so that he, Jeff, could show me a better time than Gene could afford to.

Jeff also reminded me that he knew I wanted to go to college but couldn't afford it. It seemed he knew a lot about me that he learned from Norman Jackson, one of my classmates who worked for Jeff. Norman always brought messages from Jeff to me at school. Jeff told me that if I would be his mistress (although he used the term "girl-friend"), he would pay for my college education, buy me a new car, new clothes to take with me to college, and would send me an allowance each week while I was in school. All he wanted was for me to promise to spend my summer vacations and holidays with him and to return to him once I had finished college.

Jeff was the same age as my father or older, and he looked it. He was married and his wife was a skinny, light-skinned woman who often worked in the drive-in with him. Dear's house was just around the corner from the drive-in and sometimes, when I hadn't eaten, I would stop by the drive-in for a hamburger or a hot dog. The price was reasonable and the food was good.

Once I went to the front of the drive-in to pay the cashier. Jeff told her to leave and he started operating the cash register. I gave him my money, but he refused to accept it. Instead, he took some money from his shirt pocket, put it into the cash register, and then handed me the change. I couldn't refuse it because his wife was looking and I didn't want to start any trouble. I took the money, and on my way out the door I gave it to one of the waitresses and told her to give it back to Jeff, because he had given me too much change.

I listened to the line Jeff was giving me on the phone that night, then I hung up. When I returned to my seat, Gene asked if anything was wrong. I told him I would tell him about the call later. I knew I was not going to let Jeff pay for my education, nor was I going to take money from him for anything.

Now I found myself in Gene's car on the parking lot of the drive-in telling him about Jeff and his "campaign" to make me his woman. I told Gene the story because, in my desperation and confusion, I had begun to think that perhaps I was a fool. Why should I be tortured mentally by Dear, lack of finances, and nowhere to live when I was being offered a solution to my troubles. Why didn't I cash in on my looks so that I wouldn't have to worry again about material things.

After all, the only thing Jeff wanted from me was to be his lover. What was wrong with that? I asked myself, "Was it so bad? What was worse? My current situation, or having it all? People did it all the time. Why should I be any different? I could have money in my pockets and new clothes too. I could live in a nice apartment, and I wouldn't have to worry about the rent. I could spend more time studying and wouldn't have to worry about working." Gene listened to me without a word. I ranted on and on, trying to convince myself that I should accept Jeff's offer.

Norman had often told me what a fool I was trying to work and take care of myself on nothing when Jeff was rich and could give me anything I wanted. Norman would ask, "You see that big Cadillac Jeff is driving? He said he would buy you any kind of car you wanted if you would be his woman. I don't know why women are such fools. You are sitting on a money-maker and you won't cash in on it. If I was in your place, I would jump at the chance and know that I could have anything I wanted and wouldn't have to work for it." I listened to Norman and, I must admit, that I had frequently thought along those lines, but something inside me would not let me do that.

I began to wonder if I was a fool and was perhaps being too proud. I had told Janie about Jeff's offer and she agreed that I didn't need that type of man or his money. She said, "Barbran, you're not that kind of girl. How will you face yourself if you go with him? Someone else can handle that kind of relationship, but you and I can't because we are not that kind. You and I want so much out of life, but we want to be proud of the way we get it. Years from now you will hate yourself if you become his woman."

"Anyway," she continued, "the way that Jeff feels about you, you will have to come home every holiday to be with him. And what makes you think he won't be jealous of the younger men that you will meet in college and then make you stop going to school if you can't find one closer to home so that you can be with him every weekend. And what will you say when you pray? I thought about all of the things he can give you and I know they sound exciting, but when you finish college, you can buy them for yourself, and you won't need his money or him."

As I sat in the car talking, I thought about what Janie had said. Still Gene didn't say a word. When I stopped talking and we sat silently for awhile Gene asked, "Have you finished?"

"Yes."

"I agree with Janie. You are not that kind of girl. If you were, I would have asked you a long time ago to move in with me. But, I didn't because I knew that you would have taken it as an insult. I respect you too much to disrespect you. You are a very beautiful, intelligent, ambitious, and determined young lady and I am so proud to call you my sweetheart."

He continued, "The person I just listened to is not the girl I know and love. You are talking about trying to become someone you are not and you will grow to hate that person. I know you are having a difficult time in your life right now and perhaps you feel that you are alone in the world, but remember, you will always have Janie and me. We will never turn our backs on you and we will never see you go cold or hungry."

Then he said, "You are having it hard right now, but God does not put more on us than we can bear. I don't want to tell you what to do, so let's go to church Sunday and talk to God. After that, if you still want to live with someone and can't handle the troubles and problems by yourself, move in with me and let me take care of you. I would rather do that than see you in the hands of someone like Jeff, who will ruin your life. Promise me you won't make any decision until after we have come back from church."

I asked, "What about Dear? I told her I would give her my answer tomorrow."

"Tell her you are working something out and you will let her know before the day is over."

The following day Gene and I went to church together. During the service we sat and cried freely and openly. Afterwards, we walked together, discussed the events of the previous day, and made decisions about how they should be handled.

I realized that my two good friends, Janie and Gene, who cared for me were right. I wasn't that kind of girl and I knew that eventually

I would hate myself if I became someone I didn't respect. I was ashamed of myself for even thinking of doing such a thing, and I loved Gene and Janie even more for sticking by me and for being honest with me. I was brought up in church, and I had been taught always to put my trust and faith in God and He would answer my prayers.

When we returned to Dear's house, Gene waited for me outside while I went in to tell her my decision. Dear was in the kitchen talking to one of her tenants. It was obvious they were talking about me because of their hushed tones, and they abruptly stopped talking and looked guilty when I entered the room. That didn't bother me as it had in the past. I felt a sort of calmness. I knew what I was going to tell Dear and somehow I didn't care what she thought or said about it. I felt I could deal with anything.

I said, "Dear, may I speak with you in private, please?" She didn't answer. She gave a funny look to the woman with whom she had been talking, walked out of the kitchen, and went into her bedroom. I followed her and as we entered her room I began talking.

I said, "Dear, I have given a lot of thought to what you said yesterday. I couldn't make the decision so I left it to God. I don't want to live with someone I don't know. I moved here with you until I finish school, because I felt that you would be kind to me and treat me the same way that you would want my mother to treat your child if he or she needed help. My family has known your family for many years. Janie is as close to me as my own sister."

Then I said, "Your brother [Janie's father] has been like my father from the first day I met him. Mrs. Maggie, [Janie's mother] has always treated me like her own daughter. I have slept at her house, and if I am there at dinner time, she doesn't ask me if I am hungry, she just sets a place for me at the table, just as she does for the rest of the family. I want to stay here until I graduate, but I won't beg you to let me stay; and I won't be your maid. If you still want me to leave, I will move out today. With God's help, I know I can make it."

Without giving her a chance to answer, I turned and walked out of the room. Gene was sitting on the front steps waiting for me. When I walked onto the porch he asked, "How did it go?"

I answered, "I don't know, she didn't say."

Just at that moment, Dear walked onto the porch. She had heard Gene's question and my response. She said, " I didn't say because you didn't give me a chance to say anything. I'll say one thing for you, you've got a lot of guts for someone so young. If you've got enough heart to go it alone without knowing where you are going to sleep the next night, then I have enough heart to help you. You have really made me ashamed of myself. You are welcome to stay here as long as it is necessary and I don't have any doubts in my mind; I know that you will achieve whatever you strive for in life. If I had a daughter, I would want her to be just like you."

I put my arms around her neck and she began to cry as she hugged me. I stayed with Dear until it was time for me to leave for college.

I had applied for a loan from an organization called the Parker and Hatman Education Fund. It was a private organization funded by a white millionaire. The fund was to assist deserving high school students who couldn't afford a college education. Janie and I both applied for a loan from the organization. We had to pass very difficult tests before we could be considered for financial assistance.

Later we learned that white students who applied for the loans were not required to take any tests at all. I wasn't notified if I had gotten the loan until the day that I was to leave for school. Janie didn't have any trouble getting the loan. She had a mother and father who both worked and aunts and uncles who cosigned for her. I didn't have anyone to cosign for me.

I talked to some of my teachers about where I could get money for college, because, without cosigners, I wouldn't be able to get funding from the P&H Foundation. One of my teachers, Mr. Thomas, overheard me and asked to speak with me.

We went into his classroom and he said, "I hear that you are having problems getting financing for college."

I answered, "Yes, I am but I haven't given up."

Then he said, "I'll cosign for you." He had so much faith in me that he talked another teacher, Mr. Spencer, into cosigning for me as well.

Mr. Thomas said, "Barbara, the best thing for you is to leave Columbus and go away to school. I know that you have had it hard here and I admire you more than any student I've ever met. Maybe a change of environment will make things a little easier for you."

I was very proud to have his trust. I knew that he meant what he said because cosigning for the loan meant that if I did not repay the money, or if I did not go to college, he and the other teacher would be responsible for repaying the loan.

Janie had decided to go to Lincoln University in Jefferson City, Missouri, because she had relatives who lived there, and they were willing to assist her financially. I had applied to Syracuse University in New York and to Ohio State University, because I had relatives both in Ohio and in New York. I also applied to Morgan State College (now University) in Baltimore, Maryland.

When I contacted my aunts in Ohio and New York and told them I hoped to come there for college, they said that they were very sorry, but they couldn't help me. My aunt in Ohio, actually my mother's aunt and my great-aunt, said that her husband was sick and she couldn't take care of anybody's children. She was very sorry and wished there was something she could do, but she said, "Times are hard, Honey, but I wish you the best of luck."

My aunts in New York, Mother's sisters, all said they were working and too busy to take care of a child. I was going to college, not elementary school. I was accustomed to taking care of myself, but even so, they still wouldn't help me. The loan covered my tuition only. It didn't pay for travel, room and board, or books. I hoped that if I could stay with my relatives and find a part-time job, I could make it.

Evidently, one of my aunts in New York had said something to Maelizzie about my asking if I could live with her, because one day, in a very angry tone, Maelizzie said to me, "I don't know why you keep bothering folks about staying with them. Folks got their own problems and their own lives to live. Ain't nobody got no time to look after somebody else's young-uns. I don't know why you just don't leave folks alone. Always talking 'bout college. You need to git yourself a job and find you a place to live. I don't know why that old piece of paper (meaning my high school diploma) ain't enough for you. You ain't got no money to be going to no college like white folks." I realized right then and there that the only person I could depend upon was me.

Jesse Torrance and I had been sweethearts from the time I was in the tenth grade and he was in the eleventh. He had been my date for my junior prom and we had gone steady for two years before I met Gene. Everyone, including Mother, thought that eventually Jesse and I would marry.

When he graduated from high school, he enlisted in the air force and was stationed at Fort Bragg. It was after he went to Fort Bragg that I met Gene and began dating him. Whenever Jesse came home on leave, I dated him and when he left, I dated Gene. Mother and Sandy liked Jesse better than they did Gene. Mother always said that Gene was too mature for me. After all, he had finished college and was a lieutenant in the air force, whereas I was just a high school senior.

While home on leave, Jesse had put a luggage set on lay-away at a local department store as a graduation present for me. He had given his best friend, Charles, the balance of the payment so that I would have the luggage by graduation.

When my relatives in Ohio and New York didn't want me to come to live with them and go to college, I chose Morgan State in

Baltimore. I didn't have enough money to pay the train fare to Baltimore, but I knew I would get it somehow before I had to leave, but I didn't know how. Morgan State had sent me a letter confirming my acceptance. However, I didn't know that I should also receive a "Permit to Register" notice.

Janie left for college the day before I was to leave. It was so lonely without her. But I didn't have time for self-pity. I had to get busy because I was to leave the following day and not only did I not have money for train fare, I didn't have luggage. I went to the school to tell Charles that I didn't want the luggage Jesse had put on lay-away for me. Instead, I needed the money Jesse had given him to pay for my fare to Baltimore.

Charles wasn't at school that day, and didn't have a telephone, so I went to his house looking for him. He wasn't home, so I left word with his sister, asking him to get in touch with me that day. In the meantime, I had to find something in which to pack my clothes. I went to the store where Jesse had laid-away the luggage set and convinced the saleslady that my parents had given me a set for graduation, so she refunded me the down payment, which was about fifteen dollars.

Gene drove me to several places trying to find an affordable suitcase large enough for my clothes. After a couple of hours, he had to go on duty, so I drove him back to the army base and kept his car. I finally found a large used army trunk in a pawn shop, but the lock was broken. I also found a suitcase large enough to hold my clothes and books, but its lock was broken as well. The salesman agreed to sell me both the trunk and the suitcase for five dollars.

Then, I bought a bunch of neckties and a piece of rope. I used the neckties to tie the suitcase closed and used the rope to tie the trunk. Mother had an old ragged suitcase that someone had given her, and she said I could use it, although it too didn't close properly and the lock was missing. With those three beat up pieces of luggage, I was ready to go.

I washed and packed my clothes and cartons of cigarettes I had gotten from the USO and had saved to take with me. I was determined to learn to smoke when I got to college. I thought it would make me look sophisticated. I didn't want the students to think I was a "little country girl."

While I was packing, I was thinking that it was pathetic that I was taking everything I owned with me. I thought about the movies I had seen and the books I had read about kids going away to college and returning home for summer vacations, and holidays. Surely they had not taken all of their possessions with them. Yet, what "home" would I return to? Who really wanted me? There was something final about my leaving.

I was to leave for Baltimore the next day. It was September 22, 1957. I was due at Morgan State on Monday, September 25, for freshman orientation. I hadn't heard from Charles. Two hours before the train was to leave, I still didn't have my fare. I drove to school to find Charles. I was desperate. I went to the office to see my former homeroom teacher, Mrs. Mack, to ask if she could help me find Charles.

When we finally found him, I told him I needed the money Jesse had given him for the luggage for my train fare to Baltimore. He said he didn't have the money because he had spent it. I panicked! I knew if I couldn't get the fare I couldn't go. Tears welled in my eyes.

I didn't want to create a scene and embarrass Charles, but Mrs. Mack must have sensed how desperate I was. She said to Charles, "That money was not yours to spend. Your friend trusted you. I am giving you permission to leave school to go and get the money. You have one hour to get it and bring it back to this office. We will both be right here waiting for you. If you don't return with it, I am going to visit your parents and tell them that you are a thief."

Charles looked terrified and left the campus running to get the money. Mrs. Mack told me to go and finish everything I had to do and then return to school in one hour for the money. I left not knowing what to expect when I returned, but I didn't have time to worry about it. I went back to Dear's house, finished packing, took a bath, and dressed.

Mother had bought me a charcoal-gray, two-piece dress that was gathered around the waist, with a jacket. I had gone to the beauty parlor that week, and my hair looked very good, I thought. The natural high that we as a people experience now when we refer to our "blackness" did not exist in those days. As a matter of fact, the only people of our race who were accepted by the white race as well as by members of the Negro race, were those who were most nearly white.

Those were the individuals with fair complexions, thin lips, and long hair, "good hair" it was called, "light skin with good hair." That didn't describe me. People were into using bleaching creams on the skin to lighten it, and "straightening combs" (now referred to as hot combs) and hot hair curlers to look as close to white as possible. We also used the darkest makeup that we could find. The most popular lipstick colors were the deep shades of raspberry or grape.

I put the dark makeup on my face, put on the Red Fox stockings, made sure that the dark seams up the back of my legs were straight, put the dark lipstick on my lips, combed the tight curls in my hair into a suitable style and went back to school to get my ticket money from Charles. When I got there, Charles was sitting in the principal's office waiting for me. He said he had borrowed money to replace what he had spent. I didn't want to get him in trouble, because he was a very nice boy. I just needed ticket money and he was my only source.

I hugged Mrs. Mack and thanked her for understanding and helping me get the money. I looked at Charles, and said, "I'm sorry."

He looked at me for a long time, then he put out his hand to shake mine. I could have sworn I saw tears in his eyes as he said, "You don't owe me an apology. I owe you one. I'm sorry and you are SOME lady." I hugged him and ran from the office before anyone could see me cry. I went back to Dear's house, said my good-byes and thank-yous and left to say good-bye to my family.

I drove to Maelizzie's house, but no one was there. Mother was at work. I don't remember where Sandy was. My baby brother, Al, who was three years old and the apple of my eye, ran to meet me with outstretched arms. I felt sad and disappointed that my family was not there to share this most important day in my life. I asked Maelizzie for five dollars so that I would have at least some money to buy food on the long trip. She said she didn't have any money. I didn't reply. I told her to tell Mother and Sandy good-bye for me and that I would write to them.

As I was leaving, little Al tried to follow me. When I told him that he couldn't go, he began to cry and said in his cute, babyish way, "I wanna doe wib Bobba." I picked him up, squeezed him, and cried. At least, I thought, someone will miss me. My baby brother will miss me. Somehow I knew that I would never hold him as a baby in my arms again.

Gene was waiting for me at the bus station. He had taken the bus from the post into town. He knew I would be running late, and I was. My bags were already packed and in the trunk of the car. Gene drove me to the station and checked my trunk for me. Because the suitcases didn't have locks, I was not allowed to check them through and I had to carry them onto the train with me.

Boy, I was a sight with that rope and those neckties tied around my luggage. Gene didn't comment about the shabbiness of my luggage. He looked at me and said what I had heard before, "Lady, you got a lot of guts," and he hugged me.

I needed more than guts. I needed money. But I was too proud to ask him for that. I couldn't let him know that I was destitute. Perhaps if he offered me money, I would have accepted it. But I couldn't ask. Still, I knew that had I asked, he would have given it to me gladly, but my pride got in the way.

I had just enough money for a one-way ticket to Baltimore. After I bought my ticket, I had exactly two dollars left. I knew that it was going to take me almost two days to get there. I also knew that it would be a long, hard trip without any food. I had not eaten at all that day.

Gene kissed me goodbye and we promised to write each other. He also promised to come to Baltimore to see me. I knew, deep within me, that we would never see each other again. I think he knew it, too. We stood there, holding each other for a long time. We waved as the train pulled out of the station.

The conductor pointed to my shabby bags and said, "I hope they make it."

I smiled and said "They will. They have to. I have no other choice."

Gene had stored my two pieces of luggage in the overhead compartments. I took a window seat and settled down for the long ride. I knew I wouldn't arrive until Sunday and that I wouldn't have anything to eat until Monday. I didn't know how much a taxi fare would cost from the train station to the college. Thinking about these things made me hold on to the only two dollars I had left. I had to change trains in Atlanta and I had no idea how I was going to pay someone to help me with my luggage since it was too heavy for me to carry alone.

There were four young soldiers in the same compartment with me. They had been stationed at Fort Benning and were returning home to Washington, DC and to Baltimore. They had some candy and cookies and they shared a piece of candy with me. I refused their offer to buy me lunch or anything to eat or drink, although my stomach was growling with hunger pains.

I didn't want anyone to know that I was broke and hungry. I suspected that the soldiers knew. They could not help but know; my stomach was growling so loudly that anyone sitting near me in the compartment would have to hear it. One of the soldiers asked me why

I wasn't eating. I lied and said that I had an upset stomach and didn't want to eat.

After an hour or so, the air conditioning in the car compartment broke down. I began to perspire profusely. The windows wouldn't open, so no air was circulating. My head was so sweaty that my hair looked "nappy." My makeup began to run. I looked and felt awful and my stomach was crying louder than ever. I stood up to go to the toilet to repair my makeup and, as I stood, the heel of my shoe caught in the hem of my dress and ripped it at the waist. I thought, "No problem, I'll just go into the toilet and pin it." Luckily, I had listened to Mother's advice to always carry a safety pin for emergencies when traveling. I was glad that I took her advice for once.

I went into the toilet and repaired my makeup as best as I could. As I was walking out the door, the back of my dress caught in it and the dress ripped almost completely off at the waist. I didn't have another pin. There I was, with my dress hanging off, my makeup streaked and sweaty, my hair curling up in little tight, damp knots, and my stomach growling so loudly you could hear it over the noise of the rattling train. I collapsed into my seat and cried.

The tears ruined my makeup for good, but I couldn't stop crying. I cried very softly so that no one could hear me. I was glad that I wasn't sharing my seat. I was worried about how I was going to keep my dress together. When the conductor passed by, I asked him for a few safety pins and used them to pin the dress to my slip.

I must have been a sight to see, and I still had to change trains in Atlanta. I had checked the trunk which left me with the two suitcases tied with neckties. They were so ragged that each was cracking down the middle. The conductor helped me struggle with the luggage to the platform where I waited for the next train. I looked like Little Raggedy Ann, but at that point, I didn't care. I just kept saying to myself, "The best is yet to come."

The soldiers who had been so friendly were nowhere to be found. They had hurried off the train before me. I didn't know how long it would take the next train to come and I couldn't inquire at the information booth because I couldn't carry my bags. I was afraid that if I left them, someone would think that they were trash and remove them to make way for other passengers. I reasoned that it was best to stand there with my bags. Anyway, we looked alike, my luggage and I.

When the train finally arrived, after what seemed to me like an eternity but had really been only thirty minutes, the conductor assisted me aboard with my luggage. He said, "I'll take care of the bags, Miss. You go and find a seat."

I sat next to a window and I was lucky again to get a seat without having to share it. I was glad because I didn't feel like conversation. The young soldiers had disappeared. I guessed they didn't want to be seen with me, my luggage, and my dress. I didn't blame them. I probably would have felt the same way. Smelling their food had made my stomach complain louder and louder. I guess they were tired of listening to my stomach beg. I couldn't have foreseen that, years later, I would again meet one of those soldiers through a friend, and that he and I would become friends.

A Taste of College

When I finally arrived in Baltimore, I had exactly one dollar left. I had gotten so hungry during the long trip that I bought a piece of candy on the train. When I got up to gather my luggage together as the train was pulling into the station, my shoe caught again in the hem of my dress. This time the heel put a hole in the skirt. By then, I didn't care how I looked. No matter what else might happen, I knew I couldn't look any worse than I already did.

I searched for my necktied-suitcases and finally found them, hidden behind some seats at the back of the compartment. The conductor had taken them from the overhead racks to hide them from the other passengers.

He explained, "I don't want to hurt your feelings, Miss, but they do look a little rough." I understood and wasn't hurt. "Rough" was a kind word for them. Actually they looked horrible but I couldn't do any better and they had served their purpose. I struggled with the heavy bags myself getting off the train. They were so heavy and I was so very tired, weak, and hungry.

When I finally got a taxi, I asked the driver how much it would be to get to Morgan State College. He said that the fare was usually about two dollars. I told him that I only had a dollar and asked him to take me as far as that would carry me and I would walk the rest of the way. Tears were welling up in my eyes and my lips were trembling, but I was determined that the driver wouldn't see me cry. "The worst is over," I kept telling myself. "You are here in Baltimore."

I tried hard to seem nonchalant. There I was in front of Penn station; I didn't know anyone in Baltimore; I was sweated out completely and my hair was matted to my head (this was years before the "natural" look was fashionable); all of my makeup had sweated off; the skirt of my dress was held on by large safety pins; I had punched holes in my stockings pulling on them because they were a size too small; the luggage beside me was tied together with men's neckties; my stomach was growling so loudly that people next to me moved; I had one dollar in my pocket; and I had no idea where the campus was located.

The cab driver looked at me and said, "Young lady, you look as if you have had a pretty rough trip. Where are you coming from?"

When I explained what happened on the train, he said, "You sure have a lot of guts. But right now you look like you could use a friend. I'll tell you what I'll do, I will take you to the Morgan campus for ninety cents. That will leave you a dime for a telephone call if you need it."

I was grateful to that kind old man. I did need a dime to call the train station later because my trunk hadn't arrived at the baggage room when I inquired about it. I had no idea how I would get back down to the station for my trunk when it finally did arrive, but I decided to worry about that later. The kind cab driver took me to the campus. When I got there I was told that there wasn't a room waiting for me.

I didn't know that I was to have received a "Permit to Register" notice from the college. Once I had returned the permit, I would have been guaranteed a room in one of the women's dormitories.

Mrs. Spellman, the Dean of Women, gave me a room temporarily in Tubman House. However, I wasn't to stay there because the room was already reserved for another student who had not yet arrived. To compound my troubles, I learned that nineteen dollars were supposed to have been paid at the time of registration for matching curtains and a bedspread for the dorm room. All the rooms were to be uniformly decorated.

I didn't have nineteen dollars and, even if they did find me a room, I couldn't stay without paying the nineteen dollars. Mrs. Spellman made that very clear to me. I had no idea how I would get the money. Then I thought about calling Moochie, my real father.

I used the dime I had left to call Moochie. Somehow I felt better, because I was sure that he would be proud that his only child had made it to college, and had never asked him for money before. I felt sure that he would help me, but Lucy, his wife, answered the phone. Lucy's skin was so light that she could pass for white. She never did like me. I was born long before Moochie met her. Both he and my mother were teenagers when I was born, but Lucy was still jealous of that long ago love.

The operator told Lucy that I was calling and asked if she would accept the charges. Lucy replied, "No, I don't accept telephone calls from women calling my husband."

I could hear Lucy talking to the operator and I cut in saying, "Operator, tell that woman that her husband is my father and I am not some woman calling him. I am his daughter."

Then Lucy said, "I don't recognize illegitimate children. As far as I am concerned, she is just a no-good bastard child and I don't want her calling my house disturbing my husband anymore." Then she slammed down the receiver.

The operator said, "I know that we are not supposed to interfere with our customers' business, but if it is your father whom you are calling, that woman must be crazy for not letting you speak with him. If you want me to, I'll put the call through to her again and then I will call the dormitory. If a child is trying to go to school, we adults should try to help as much as we can. I am mad as hell with that woman and I have never laid eyes on her. I was an illegitimate child too and I understand how you feel, Honey. Don't you cry and don't let that stupid woman make you lose faith in yourself."

I thanked her for those kind words because I sure needed them at that moment. I told her not to call Lucy back, to let the matter drop. I knew it would be futile. I hung up the phone and went back to my temporary room.

I went in, lay across the bed, and started to cry. All the other students were preparing to go to dinner. I didn't have any money, nor did I have a meal ticket. Had the required Permit to Register arrived before I came to Morgan, I would have received a meal ticket and I would have at least been able to eat. However, I didn't know about that at the time I left. I was just glad to be leaving Georgia and glad that I had been accepted by Morgan.

God, I was so hungry and so depressed. I felt as if I didn't have a friend in the world. The operator's message kept running through my head. I knew she was right and I kept saying over and over to myself, "One day I am going to look back on all of this and laugh."

Lola, my roommate, saw me crying and hugged me without asking any questions. There was a room reserved for her but for some reason it was not quite ready. She and I became friends quickly. She was easy to talk to and I talked freely with her about my troubles. I told her about my arrival at Morgan State and about the troubles I had encountered, not only trying to get there but also trying to stay there.

She listened silently, and kept shaking her head slowly from side to side saying, "Ummmmmmm, I don't know how you did it. I would have said 'fuck it all,' a long time ago and let that man, what's his name, Jeff, take care of me. I would not have gone through all that shit like you did. I can't help but to admire you. Girl, you sure got a lot of heart. That's all I can say." I knew that not many people would understand why I did what I did, but I had to do it my way.

All meals were served in what was called the refectory. Lola called her mother and told her that she had left one of her suitcases at home in Virginia and she needed it now. Her mother said she would bring the suitcase later that day. When she arrived, Lola had already left for the refectory. She must have told her mother about my troubles when she phoned home, because when her mother came into the room and saw me lying across the bed in the dark room crying, she walked over to me, put her hand on my shoulder and said, "Don't cry, Honey. It'll all work out."

Then she walked out of the room. When I turned over, I saw three dollars on the bed beside me. I was so glad. I needed the money to pay cab fare to go to the train station to get my trunk. I was glad that she left the money without asking me if I needed it, because I would have said no. My pride wouldn't have allowed me to admit that I really needed the three dollars.

I found some other girls who also needed to return to the train station to get their luggage. We decided to go together in one cab and split the fare between us. When we returned to campus, the driver refused to help us carry our luggage to the basement of Holmes Hall, where all luggage was stored. I knew I couldn't carry my heavy trunk down those stairs so I stood at the top of the steps to the basement, gave the trunk a good push, and let it slide down the steps. It didn't pop open, which surprised me because it was so torn and thin from years of use.

When it was clear that I couldn't get the nineteen dollars for the curtains and bedspread, Dean Spellman told me about the "Approved

Homes" program. An approved home was one located in a nice residential area that had been inspected and checked thoroughly by the college prior to assigning student occupants; however, the inspection was not always thorough. Dean Spellman once again stressed that under no circumstances would I be permitted to live in a dormitory without first paying nineteen dollars. She said that the approved homes frequently included board for Morgan students.

After being at Morgan for a couple of days, I was transferred to an "approved home." It was the home of a Mrs. Watkins, a very religious lady, who was active in the NAACP and other community organizations. She was a short little woman with gray hair, and she took an immediate dislike to me. She was a beautician and worked from a salon in the basement of her home on Gilmore Street.

Margie, a student from New York, who also arrived at Morgan State without a reserved room, and I were to room together at Mrs. Watkins's house. We shared the taxi to the Gilmore Street address.

I remember the first time I saw Gilmore Street. When the taxi stopped in front of Mrs. Watkins's house, I was so disappointed that I got out of the cab, looked around at the dirty streets, and cried. The streets were littered with trash. It wasn't that the streets were filthy, but there was more trash on the curbs and sidewalks than I was accustomed to seeing in the South.

We struggled to get the trunk inside Mrs. Watkins's house; this time the taxi driver helped. When we got it just inside the front door, the entire bottom fell out of the trunk. I pulled the contents out and carried them upstairs by hand. Later, I used the trunk to store things I wouldn't use immediately.

Margie and I were to share a tiny room and one large bed on the third floor of Mrs. Watkin's house. Margie had light brown skin and was short and stocky like Mrs. Watkins, and she was always giggling. Margie would sit and talk about her family problems with Mrs. Watkins. Although Mrs. Watkins often questioned me about my personal life, I wouldn't discuss it with her and she construed this to be a sign of rebellion and unfriendliness. Margie's father sent her money every week, but no one sent me any. Already, I didn't fit in.

I usually stayed on campus later than Margie so that I could study in the library. My grades were better than Margie's, but Mrs. Watkins always accused me of staying out with "some man."

Mrs. Watkins frequently took me into what she called the "prayer room," to scold me about something I had done or something she thought I had done. This room held a huge open Bible on a white podium at the center of the room. There were figurines of Jesus, religious posters, candles around the room, and poems pinned up on the walls. We were required to remove our shoes before entering the room.

I don't know why Mrs. Watkins didn't trust me. I had never lied to her and she didn't know anything about me. Margie was constantly lying to Mrs. Watkins about her social life and she was slipping out almost every night to see a bus driver she was dating. Nevertheless, Mrs. Watkins believed her when she said she was going to visit some friends on campus.

One day I got sick in class and began coughing uncontrollably. The instructor sent me to the infirmary. The infirmary doctor said that because I was an out-of-state student living in an approved home rather than with relatives, I was to be treated as if I were living on campus. That meant confinement in the clinic so that the college could be sure that I was receiving proper treatment. Mrs. Watkins called to verify that I was not lying after I called to tell her that I was sick and confined to the campus clinic.

It was while I was living with Mrs. Watkins that I met Jerry, who was to become my husband. One September night in 1957, when I had not been long at Morgan, I was feeling sorry for myself, as I often did when I thought about home and felt alone in the world. It seemed as if everyone at Morgan had a sweetheart, except me. Everyone talked about receiving packages from home, except me. Everyone looked forward to going home for the Christmas holidays, except me. I often sat eating in the cafeteria and pretending someone was waiting for me at home.

That night, after staying late on campus, listening to John Coltrane alone in a soundproof booth on the second floor of the library, I walked to the bus stop, about three blocks away. As I walked up the dark street, I noticed a man walking behind me carrying what I thought were books.

Actually, they were record albums of jazz musicians such as Coltrane, Ella Fitzgerald, Charlie Parker, and others. I thought he must be a fellow student and, because I didn't like walking alone, I slowed my pace to allow him to catch up with me. We exchanged pleasantries and walked to the bus stop together. He told me that his name was Jerry and that he wasn't married. Later I learned that he was married and the father of a baby daughter, but he and his wife were separated at that time.

I gave him Mrs. Watkin's phone number and address and he started calling me. A few weeks later, I asked him to a party given by a girl in my English class that weekend. After that we began to date regularly. He was very handsome and was accustomed to dating lots of different women. I got to know most of his friends, who seemed to always be drinking and having a good time.

I fell in love with Jerry. He was a man, so different from the boys I had dated. He played golf, smoked a pipe, dressed very well, frequented the best nightclubs and restaurants in town, had his own apartment, always had plenty of money to spend, and he was exciting because he knew so many colorful characters like gamblers and hustlers.

That kind of life was something I had only read about. He was older than I, a man-about-town, and I liked the way he paid attention to me when we were out together. He treated me as if I were the only woman in the room and I blossomed with that attention, because I had been so neglected at home.

Mrs. Watkins didn't like Jerry so I had to sneak out, pretending to go to the store or to the campus to study when we would meet. I was getting fed up with the way Mrs. Watkins was treating me. I had been on my own too damned long to be sneaking out of a place where I was paying rent. I went to the Dean of Women to ask her to please find me another place to stay. She found me another approve home where the owner was an alcoholic woman. Margie wanted to move out with me, but Mrs. Watkins called her father and he threatened to make her come home if she moved, so I moved alone.

My new roommate was Doris. The tiny room we shared was barely large enough for one person. I'm sure that if someone from the college had seen the size and the condition of that room, students would not have been permitted to live there. The room had no windows, and no heat. We slept together on a single cot. The bathroom was on another floor and to get there we had to cross through another lodger's room. We had to hang our clothes outside our room behind a door in the hallway. The conditions were horrible.

The woman was Mrs. Diggs, the widow of a prominent doctor. When she was younger she must have been a very beautiful woman, but alcohol and time had left their marks on her.

I was spending more time with Jerry than I was at Mrs. Diggs's house. When the Dean called me to her office, I thought that Mrs. Diggs had reported me. The Dean told me to move on campus because she was afraid I might get into trouble. It seems that Mrs. Watkins had called the college and told the Dean about my family problems.

When I reminded the Dean that I couldn't afford to live in the dorm, she said the college was prepared to let me live there free of charge. I felt they just wanted me to stop dating Jerry. I refused to move into the dorms and I refused to stop dating Jerry. I was told that if I did not comply, I would be expelled to avoid "giving the college a bad name."

I was told that the alternative was to withdraw from college, that way I wouldn't have the expulsion on my record. So I withdrew. I had no idea what I was going to do; but, I had my old friends, loneliness and rejection at my side again. Ironically, some twenty-four years in the future, a judge, like the Dean, would ask me to resign or be fired. The Dean had said "expelled," which is the same thing as "fired." Each time I was to make it over the hurdles.

A few months after Jerry and I had been dating, I discovered that I was pregnant. In those days single pregnant women couldn't go to college. I wouldn't have been able to continue anyway, because I had withdrawn and my grant money would soon stop. Jesse, the boy I dated in high school and the source of the money that got me to Baltimore in the first place, might have helped me then, but he had stopped trying to get in touch with me.

He had called me several times while I was living with Mrs. Watkins. He had written almost every day. He had even come to Baltimore to find me and had gone to Mrs. Watkins's house and left messages for me, saying he had rented a room around the corner and that he wanted to marry me. After I met Jerry, I forgot all about Jesse and I guess he had just stopped trying.

I tried everything short of abortion. When I still didn't menstruate, I went to New York with Margie for the summer vacation. I hoped to find a summer job and get an abortion while I was in New York. I found work in Hempstead, Long Island as a mother's helper. It was a live-in job. I missed Jerry and I wanted to go back to be with him. I was afraid of an abortion. They were often performed in filthy rooms with unsterilized equipment in the hands of unskilled people.

The woman who was scheduled to perform my abortion had aborted a young girl the previous week and the girl subsequently bled to death. Over the phone, I told Jerry of my fears and he said to return to Baltimore and we would work it out together. I hurried back and we went apartment hunting. He already had a nice apartment with nice furniture, but the furniture had been his and his wife's. I didn't want it in our apartment. I wanted our own. Jerry understood and he returned the furniture to the store.

We didn't have time to wait for Jerry's divorce, because I wanted to re-enroll in college, but I needed a marriage license. Jerry had said he was going to marry me whether his wife contested the divorce or not. "I don't care what she says. I am going to marry you," he said and he did marry me before he divorced his first wife.

We were married by a justice of the peace in Virginia. Jerry had to work that night, so we went back to his apartment where I waited for him. I was so miserable being alone on my wedding night. As soon as we were married it seemed my entire life changed into a living hell.

TRAUMA

People often asked me why I tried so hard to get good grades in school. Why did I spend so much time reading? Even after I was a married woman with children of my own, I pursued education. An older good friend once asked me, "What drives you? Why do you keep trying to earn college degrees? I'm not saying that you should not pursue a college education, but you have been in school as long as I have known you. What is it that drives you so hard? Why don't you rest awhile and spend some time with your family? Don't you think that you deserve to take some time for yourself?"

She was right, of course. I did need to spend time with my husband and children, but the truth was, I never felt really loved by either my mother or my husband. The same sense of aloneness carried over from my childhood into my adult life. I felt that I had to be the best at whatever I tried so that my mother and then my husband, would be proud of me. I felt like an outsider, even in my marriage; like a little girl who would do just about anything to get attention and praise, even commit a crime or pretend to be sick or maybe become a comedian.

When I earned my undergraduate degree, I asked Jerry, "Are you proud of me now?"

He answered, "Yes siree."

That meant that I had pleased him, and pleasing him might make him love me, I hoped. I was so love-starved and lonely. I even rationalized Jerry's staying out all night so often. We lived in a little, one bedroom apartment and I would try to convince myself that he didn't have anything at home to entertain him. Therefore, he deserved to go out and be entertained.

It didn't matter that I was left alone in a cramped, hot third-floor apartment without a telephone. Nor did it matter that I knew no one in Baltimore except his friends. It didn't matter that days and sometimes weeks passed when I didn't go outside. Jerry brought in the mail when he did come home, and he bought the groceries, so there was no need for me to go downstairs. None of this seemed to matter to Jerry. Only Jerry mattered to Jerry.

After Jericka was born, I told myself that Jerry went out all the time because he didn't want to be home with a crying baby, dirty diapers, and me. That was the way it was supposed to be, I told myself. Wow, what a naive fool I was.

Jerry never came home on Friday or Saturday nights. I was pregnant; I didn't know anyone in Baltimore; I had dropped out of college; I couldn't go home; my grant had been withdrawn; and, I had no money and no job. I thought God was punishing me for lying when we exchanged our wedding vows, saying that Jerry wasn't married. Years later, after the children were born and Jerry's divorce was final, we remarried legally, in church with a minister. When we married the second time, Jerry had exactly two dimes in his pocket. I saved those dimes as a reminder of our struggle together.

At any rate, things had gotten so bad between Jerry and me that I didn't know what to do. I just knew things had to get better. I didn't have any job skills. Jerry was drinking, gambling, and running around with women. When we finally got a telephone, the women would call me on the phone and curse me out.

Once when he was out, a woman called me and said, "When your husband gets home, try to keep him at home and there won't be no damn shit." Jerry came home about an hour later with scratches on his face, as though he had been fighting with a woman.

I said, "Your woman just called and told me to try to keep you at home. Did you two have a fight?" He looked at me and walked away without answering. I guess in a way I was lucky. He didn't beat me like Frank did Mother.

I said to Jerry, "You made a mother out of me before I became mature enough to handle the responsibility."

I felt that I had become the mother of four children while still a child mentally. But the truth was, I was as much of a woman as I could ever have been at my age. Since I have found God, I realize that everything has to happen in its own time. I was not meant to be as knowledgeable when I was twenty as I was when I was forty. With age comes wisdom, at least that is the way it should be. This is not to say that younger people lack wisdom; rather, they are not wise enough to recognize that they may possess it.

We were living in the projects and I was in Jean's apartment when the telephone rang. I was always down in Jean's apartment or she was upstairs in mine. I was sitting close to her phone when it rang, so I answered it.

Jean and I were closer than many sisters. We hung out together; we lived in the same building in the projects; we each had husbands who chased other women; we each had four children; and we were about the same age. As a matter of fact, a lot of our neighbors thought we were sisters. The fact that I answered Jean's phone was not unusual, we were like family. My children called her "Aunt Jean." It was one of Jerry's friends, calling to tell me that Jerry had been shot and was in the hospital in serious condition. I rushed to my apartment to make sure that the children were all right and then I went straight to the hospital.

It was Saturday night. Provident Hospital was a black-operated hospital just one block from Pennsylvania Avenue. Pennsylvania Avenue, or "The Avenue," was where all the black nightclubs were; where the black theaters were; where the pimps, prostitutes, drug pushers and number writers hung out; where the sleazy hotels where a prostitute could rent a room for two dollars were; where gambling houses were; where the little junky stores owed and managed by white folks who sold cheap clothes and used furniture at high prices to poor black folks were; where there was killing and/or cutting every week-end; and, where the police were paid by black pushers and pimps to look the other way.

It was where the Royal Theater was. The Royal Theater was to Baltimore what the Apollo Theater was to New York City, and the Howard Theater was to Washington, DC. Every black entertainer who came to Baltimore during the `40s, `50s, and `60s performed at the Royal Theater. Baltimore had Baltimore Street, "The Block," for white night life, and Pennsylvania Avenue, or "The Avenue," for black night life.

I think every city has a Pennsylvania Avenue. In New York it's Harlem and 125th Street. In California, it's Watts. In Washington, DC, it's called 7th Street. In Columbus, Georgia, it's 8th Avenue. It's usually the place where Blacks hang out on street corners, and tell lies about how much money they are going to make or how much they have already. It's the city section where pimps and prostitutes come to turn tricks and show off their finery on the weekends. It's the city section where respectable parents don't want their children to hang out or even visit. It's the city section that every preacher talks about from the pulpit. Yet, it's the city section most fascinating to young folks because of glitter of night life and of life in the fast lane. It is the city section where young boys go to get rich. They think that dope dealers, drug pushers, and pimps are "cool" driving their big cars, wearing expensive clothes and jewelry and making lots of money.

The kids don't realize how much time their "idols" have spent in jail, and how many of them never got to enjoy youth, or, in some cases, never really enjoyed life at all. Every waking moment is spent either dodging the police or fighting to stay alive in the jungle of other "fast lane livers" who think the same way; that is, it's "cool" and "slick" to live by the gun, to live dangerously.

How can a price be put on freedom? When you are born and raised in the ghetto and are accustomed to living on food stamps; to standing in long lines for dried milk, powdered eggs, two pounds of cheese, flour, and a jar of peanut butter; to looking at men who drive big cars, wear expensive clothes and jewelry, and have lots of pretty, well-dressed women of all races hanging on their arms; that seems to be the kind of life to lead, especially to an impressionable child.

Young people don't think about the consequences of jail. They think, "That won't happen to me - that's something that happens to the other guy." No one thinks about his mother crying herself to sleep many nights from worry, wondering where her child is, or worse yet, knowing where that child is. No one thinks that one day his mother will have to sell everything she owns to get enough money to pay an attorney to try to keep her child out of jail, even though the effort may fail.

People can't imagine that a mother might be relieved when her child is finally caught and put into prison, because she prays that prison will "teach him a lesson and make a man of him." Yet, after her child is imprisoned, she worries that prison may make a "woman" out of him, or make a "man" out of her.

Provident Hospital, because of its location, was usually the hospital that received all the shooting and stabbing victims from The

Avenue. At one time, it was the only hospital that would provide quality treatment to "colored patients," and the only hospital in which "colored" doctors and nurses worked.

Division Street, where Provident was located, was a little back street in the heart of the black community. It was residential with row houses along each side of the small, narrow street. Provident Hospital was a white stone building that stood up on an embankment. I used to go in through the rear entrance. I would get off the bus on Pennsylvania Avenue and walk through the small cluttered alleys and small streets to reach the hospital. The place was always noisy and busy with people coming and going. I had never seen a white person in the hospital, not even a white doctor.

Jerry was in the operating room when I arrived. After I identified myself the nurse at the front desk told me to be seated on a long wooden bench in the waiting room. I was so scared, sitting there all alone. I thought, "What if he dies? What will the kids and I do?" Never mind how much we argued - the fact was that I loved my husband.

I sat in the waiting room and cried until there were no tears left. After what seemed like hours but had only been minutes, I looked up through my tears and saw a bunch of Jerry's friends arrive. Evidently they had been together gambling at a card party when Jerry was shot. A few minutes later, Joanie, my other close friend, came in the door. Jean had called her after I left for the hospital. Jean stayed at my apartment with my children and she had told Joanie to come to the hospital to be with me.

Joanie came over and put her arms around me and we cried together. As she hugged me tightly I cried uncontrollably. When I finally stopped, she looked at me and said, "You love him, don't you?"

"Yes, I do. I love him very much and I cannot imagine life without him."

While we waited, I watched the faces of every person who walked through the swinging doors from the operating room. I didn't know if they were doctors or nurses, but I searched the faces of every person who had on a uniform and seemed to work in the hospital, looking for a sign that might tell me how my husband was doing. I didn't want to talk; I just wanted to be alone with my grief, my thoughts, and my prayers.

I thought about how much Jerry and I had grown apart and how much I wanted just to be his wife and the mother of his children. I could remember being out in the street, alone trying not to think about who he was loving at that moment and how lonely I was; not wanting to go home to an empty bed again; knowing that he wouldn't be coming home that night; and trying to decide what to do after the bars closed at 2 a.m.

I remember praying, "Lord, I wish I could go home." But "home" would be an empty bed in a lonely apartment in the projects with the children sleeping and with no one to keep me company. It had become so much a part of my life that I never expected him to come home on weekends.

Jerry let me meet him at his job when he got paid Friday evenings, then he would give me most of his paycheck, because he knew that if he kept it, it would all be gone before he came home. He was a heavy gambler and when he would come home broke, he always said he had gambled the money away. But I suspected that he also spent a lot of it buying other women drinks in bars then going to motels with them.

He knew just about every bar in Baltimore and all the surrounding counties. He had been in most of them, especially those in remote places where he was not likely to be seen. Ask my husband about any backwoods bar or nightclub in the Washington and Maryland area, he has been there.

Jerry was with the crowd that frequented such places when he was shot. They were at his uncle Jackie's house, where they gambled every weekend. His uncle lived on a little street that was more like an alley than a street. Everyone in Jerry's crowd eventually wound up at Jackie's on weekends. Everything was available there, from liquor, to cards, to dice, and women. I had bailed Jerry out of jail more than once for gambling, fighting, or not paying his speeding tickets. He had been arrested in gambling house raids and for shooting dice in alleys.

Jerry liked that type of crowd. He had even taken some of his women to his uncle's house to spend the night. His uncle told me about Jerry using his house to sleep with other women one night when he was trying to get me to sleep with him while Jerry was in the hospital recuperating from the gunshot wound.

I sat on the cold bench at the hospital for hours that seemed like days, thinking about our mixed-up, hurting past. The operation lasted nine hours. The doctor told me that my husband was lucky to be alive. He said that Jerry had been shot in the abdomen with a .38 revolver.

The bullet went into his stomach, entered the blood stream, circled his body six times, passed through the small and large intestines and tore up everything that it hit before exiting through his back. The doctor said that there were so many holes in Jerry's large intestine that it looked as if moths had been eating it and half of it had to be removed. Jerry was indeed a very blessed man. God must have said, "It is not time."

How does one explain why some things happen? Why is it that two people can be involved in the same accident and one survives while the other does not? Only God can answer those questions. I just know that God saw fit to let my husband live to enjoy his grandchildren, and I thank Him for that blessing.

When Jerry came out of surgery he was still unconscious. The doctor told me, "But he will be all right if he makes it through the night." But I learned later that Jerry had actually seen death on that operating table. He said that when the bullet hit him it felt as if his insides were on fire. He said he kept thinking that if someone would just put out the fire, he would be all right. He was bleeding profusely.

The doctor said that the excessive bleeding was due to the amount of alcohol Jerry had consumed before he was shot; he was drunk. Jerry said he remembered being hit by the bullet and falling to the floor like a piece of limp dough.

He said a tear rolled down his cheek and he whispered softly, "Someone call the ambulance. I've been shot. Somebody please help me." He remembered being lifted and put on a stretcher and put into the ambulance. He remembered the sirens blaring as the ambulance raced through the streets. He remembered being rushed through the crowded emergency room.

Jerry said he remembered lying on the operating table. "It was cold when they were undressing me for the operation," he told me. "My body was so cold that my teeth were chattering, but I felt so hot inside my body, it was unbearable. To be both hot and cold and in so much pain is an experience that I cannot describe in words."

He said that as he lie on the operating table, he heard the doctors discussing his condition and he remembers slipping into unconsciousness, wondering about the faces that were peering down at him. One of the doctors and Jerry later became friends. He told him that when they opened his stomach and found the amount of damage the bullet had done to his intestines, they thought that it was futile to operate, believing that he would be dead in a matter of minutes, not hours, minutes.

Dr. Brown, the kind doctor who befriended Jerry, said that Jerry stopped breathing on the operating table; his heart stopped beating and they couldn't get a pulse. They tried massaging his heart and all other known techniques to restore life functions to Jerry's body. However, none worked. Just as they were about to give up and pronounce him dead, he began to breathe again.

Jerry was put on a ward with approximately twenty-four other male patients, who were aligned in four rows of six beds. When they brought him down from the operating room that first night, and I saw him with all those tubes in his arms and nose, I began to scream uncontrollably. I had never seen a man so pale, helpless, and vulnerable. They were careful not to upset the bottles containing the life-sustaining fluids and blood that were flowing into Jerry's body through those awful-looking tubes. The sheets of his bed were still covered with his blood. The nurses hadn't had time to change the bed linen after the operation.

They didn't take him into intensive care, although the operation had almost cost him his life. Instead, they wheeled him onto a ward, still unconscious and needing to be changed, with other less seriously ill patients.

I saw only the blood, the tubes, and the paleness of my husband. I covered my mouth with my hands to stifle the sobs that were fighting to exit my throat. When one of the doctors assured me that Jerry was still alive, I wanted to get away from the staring eyes and sympathetic voices so that I could cry and scream with joy that my husband was still alive, and to cry and give thanks to God for sparing him. I also wanted to cry for the pain that I imagined Jerry must have suffered.

I turned around and ran as fast as I could through the ward, past the nurses' station, past the offices, past waiting patients, up the long hallway to the front door, and down the steep steps that led to the street. The doctors tried to catch me to make sure I was all right but I was too fast for them. I always hated the smell of hospitals. There was something terrifying about them. I guess I equated hospitals with pain and death and I just wanted to get as far away from that smell as I possibly could.

The nurse assigned to the ward during the day was Miss Thompson. She was an ugly woman; tall, dark, and masculine. She reminded me of a female wrestler. She never smiled.

Jerry always talked about how Nurse Thompson worked double and triple shifts to earn extra money. I told him that was why the hospital had such a bad reputation; the nurses and the doctors were frequently so tired that they couldn't give their best to the patients. That seemed to happen in most black- operated facilities. There was never enough money for proper equipment, proper food, adequate staff, and so on.

Jerry had been close to death many other times before this incident. After such fitful nights, I would sit for hours the following day and write my thoughts into composition books and read them later. My little books were always filled with pain and loneliness.

Jerry came home after such a night stabbed and cut up badly. He had been slashed across the stomach and chest and his throat had been cut. He had already been to the hospital where the wounds had been stitched and bandaged.

Later he told me that he had been at one of the gambling joints where he was winning big. Some young strangers had seen him on a roll and had followed him outside and tried to rob him. Jerry, being the sort of man that he is, had refused their demands and tried to fight them off.

One of them pulled a switchblade and started cutting him while the other held his arms behind his back. After the attack, they robbed him and left him for dead. He managed to crawl out of the alley and someone found him and called the police and ambulance. Judging from his wounds, he was indeed lucky. I thank God for sparing him. Jerry said that he really didn't suffer because he was so drunk when it happened.

After the shooting, Jerry told the doctor that he remembered a feeling of great warmth and happiness and the pain was gone. He said that he felt weightless, he heard soft music, and he saw a soft, white light shining in the distance, just out of his reach. He could walk, and felt compelled to walk toward the light.

A door opened to reveal a burning fire and he could feel the heat. It was as if he were on an elevator and the door opened to the heat and fire. But he wouldn't get off the elevator and go to the heat; he started toward the warm, soft light, but he heard my voice in the distance calling his name saying, "Jerry, don't go. The children and I are waiting for you."

He remembered a figure dressed in white whose face he couldn't see, beckoning Jerry to him. The figure was standing in the path of soft, white light. Jerry remembered deciding not to go toward the figure but to go instead in the direction of my voice. Perhaps that was the moment when he started to breathe again. Perhaps because he loved the children and me enough to live for us, he didn't die. Perhaps God was not through with him yet.

I believe that God does everything for a purpose. Jerry is now a Christian. He is a very special, loving man. Our children worship the ground he walks on. God knew that days like today would come, but we each had to go through our growing period before we could become who God wanted us to become. Jerry has helped so many people in his life.

Perhaps God spared Jerry just so that he could help others. He didn't change over night. It took years for us to become the people that we are today. It took pain, understanding, tolerance, patience, giving, and forgiving. Jerry is convinced that he actually died and was brought back to this earthly life by God. We always felt that God had something special planned for him.

Alone and Lonely

The year that Jerry spent in the hospital was very trying for us, to say the least. I was working for a manufacturing company and didn't make much money, and I had to take care of our four children. It was difficult being in the apartment alone. Butch, our only son and the youngest, was three years old. The hospital wouldn't let him visit his father. When Jerry was strong enough to be wheeled out into the waiting room I would take the children to visit him.

Some people think that being alone and being lonely are the same, that one naturally causes the other. That is not true. A person can be lonely in a crowded room and, conversely, a person can be alone but not feel lonely. I was both alone and lonely. When I reflect on those days, I realize that I was lonely even when I was with Jerry. He was with me physically, but mentally, he seemed to be elsewhere.

I didn't really fit into his world. I wasn't a card player or a fast woman who hung out in bars. On the other hand, had I been that type of woman, I wouldn't have been his wife. He wanted a wife who stayed at home, took care of his children, cleaned his house, cooked his meals, washed and ironed his clothes, who didn't drink and didn't go out without him.

Yet, when he was in the streets, he seemed to prefer just the opposite in the women with whom he socialized. They were always loud, light-complexioned, and they hung out at nightclubs. Some of them, I later learned, were prostitutes.

I often took out my frustrations on my children. God knows I loved those kids, but at that time in my life I was the worst mother I had ever met. I actually abused my children. Oh, I didn't beat them unmercifully or excessively, or actually hurt them physically, but I sure did abuse them mentally and emotionally, especially the triplets. They were born just eight months after my first child, Jericka.

The two surviving triplets stayed in the hospital for six months before they were strong enough to come home. They were so tiny that they had to be fed intravenously through veins in their heads. I carried them inside me for eight months, not knowing that I was going to have triplets. The doctor just thought I was going to have a large baby. In fact, he had begun to scold me for gaining so much weight. In the '50s, it was unusual for a woman to have triplets. I felt blessed. When one died, I cried so hard they had to put me in a room and close the door.

The hospital called me and told me to come to the hospital right away, never saying what was wrong. When we arrived at the hospital, our daughter was dead. We didn't even have a chance to name her, but she would have been named Jeanette.

People tease me and say that I should be in *Believe It Or Not*, because I had four children within one year and they were not quads. Jericka was born in February, and the triplets were born in November of the same year. I didn't go back for my six-week check up, because I was already pregnant.

I enjoyed dressing them alike and having people admire my babies. When I heard a cry, I knew which one it was. Jerry would look at them and not know which one was which. I guess it's just something about mothers knowing their children.

I often abused my children by calling them names and cursing at them. I had one of the nastiest mouths in Baltimore. I could out-cuss the best of them and still have a vulgar vocabulary of unused cuss words left over. Any profanity I lacked, I would invent, just as Frank and Mother had done. I would curse Jerry with really vulgar, dirty words.

I would often invite him to kiss my ass and I sprinkled the invitation with additional vulgar words, as if that were not coarse enough. In later years, he and I would fight more about my telling him to kiss my ass than about anything else. I said those things to him when I was angry, which was most of the time. I loved Jerry very much and I was so jealous over him that I didn't trust anyone.

I was sad to spend Easter, Christmas, Thanksgiving and all the other holidays alone. In January, when Jerry was shot, I thought that he would be in the hospital for only a few weeks. Soon the weeks turned into months, and the months into a year.

Easter came and I was sick with a fever. I had suffered with my tonsils from childhood. My mother was told that they should be removed, but they never were. People had told me horror stories about how much harder a tonsillectomy was for older persons. Believing these stories, I just suffered whenever they flared up. This time they were really inflamed.

Around the corner from the projects was an eye, ear, nose and throat Clinic. I had been awake all night suffering with pain from my inflamed tonsils. As soon as the clinic opened the following morning, I went for help. My throat was swollen so badly that I couldn't swallow. I was very ill, but I had to go shopping for Easter clothes for the children. They were too young to be able to understand if they didn't get new Easter outfits, and the other children in the projects would have ridiculed them.

Jericka had just turned seven. She had always been very smart for her age. I called her into my bedroom and said, "Honey, Mommie is very sick and cannot go to buy Easter outfits for you and your sisters and brother."

She responded saying, "I can go shopping for them."

I smiled and said, "I know that you would if you could, but you're too young. You're just a little girl. What do you know about buying clothes?"

She said "I can learn. Miss Gladys can show me."

Gladys was our next door neighbor. In the projects there were twelve families per floor, and twelve floors in each building. The apartments were so close together that you could hear the people talking next door. I called Gladys and asked her if she would mind taking Jericka shopping.

Gladys was a very stocky woman. She had two sons at that time and later she had two daughters. Each daughter must have weighed over two hundred pounds while still a teen-ager. Gladys kept a very clean house and was always doing a little something extra for her family. Sometimes, in the summer, she would pull her kitchen table and chairs outside on the ramp and serve dinner to her family.

Robert, Gladys's husband was a tall, thin man and very handsome. He was just the opposite of Jerry. Robert was a homebody. He never went anywhere without Gladys. I envied her, because that was the kind of home I wanted. I wanted Jerry to stay home with me, or at least take me with him when he went out. But if he was going out and I tried to go with him, he would run off and leave me. I would cry, turn around, and go back home.

After a while I stopped crying, and I stopped trying to follow him. I just didn't care anymore. I realized that I had something to offer in my own right. He might have been looking at someone else, but maybe someone else was looking at me. Gladys often said that she didn't know how our marriage lasted, because we were both pulling in different directions. Because marriage was a partnership, we should both pull together.

Jerry and I often listened to Gladys's advice because she was our elder. But it hurt me to know that everyone knew about Jerry's affairs with other women. I hated to have anyone feel sorry for me. I never could accept pity; it was so degrading. I thought that if I were to go out, maybe people would stop pitying me.

I also wanted to feel that I was still desirable and attractive. When a woman is left at home all the time with only her children as company, not going to the beauty salon, not buying new clothes, and seldom meeting professional people, she begins to wonder if she may have lost whatever she had that attracted her husband. I wanted reassurance and attention. Jerry was giving his to others. I always wondered why. Why did he need anyone else? I felt so insecure with our marriage.

The man who shot Jerry was named Willie, and he was a friend of Jerry's. The shooting was an accident. Willie promised Jerry that he would take care of the children and me, as if we were his own family, until Jerry was well and able to take care of us himself. Therefore, Willie gave me money to buy the children's Easter clothes. Because I was too sick to go, Gladys took Jericka shopping. Although Jericka was very young, she had to assume the role of the mother.

Gladys and Jericka returned with some beautiful clothes. Because Gladys had only boys, she didn't have experience shopping for little girls. I learned later that Jericka had made the selections. I was so proud of my daughter, but that was typical of her. She has always made me proud.

During my illness, I awoke one morning to a quiet apartment. I felt uneasy because I didn't hear the children. I knew they couldn't go to school that day, because I was too sick to comb their hair and prepare their clothes for school. They also hadn't had breakfast, because I was too sick to get out of bed to prepare it.

I heard what sounded like sweeping. I struggled to get out of bed, but I was too weak and I fell over backwards onto the bed. I tried again and that time I made it. I found Jericka sweeping the kitchen and hallway. I asked where the other children were. She answered, "The twins are in school and Butchie is in nursery school."

I asked how they got ready for school. I thought perhaps one of the neighbors had come to help.

She said, "I combed the twins' hair, ironed their dresses, and gave them breakfast."

I said, "Don't worry, Baby. Mommie will be all right. You get dressed and go to school."

She said, "I got to take care of you. Even if you beat me, I still won't leave you. You might die 'cause ain't nobody here to take care of you but me." I hugged her real tight, kissed her, and got back into bed, crying and thanking God for my little daughter who was wise beyond her seven years.

That was just like Jericka. One night I came home to discover that the babysitter had left the children alone. When I walked into the apartment, it was filled with smoke. The curtains around the kitchen sink had burned completely off and Jericka was running back and forth from the bathroom to the kitchen carrying a small glass to get water from the bathroom sink to pour on the burning curtains, and shouting instructions to her sisters and brother.

When everything was under control, I asked her how the fire had started and she told me that the twins had been playing with matches. At the tender age of five, she had enough sense not to panic and to know how to put out the fire and protect her sisters and brother. She knew not to use the faucet at the kitchen sink for water to put out the fire.

Now that I am much older and the children are all grown, I realize how lucky I am to have such beautiful, intelligent children. When I was younger, they were a hindrance to me; I wanted my freedom. I wanted a good time and they were too much of a responsibility for me. God, if I had my life to live over again I would cherish those nights when my children put their arms around my neck, kissed me good night, and said, "I love you, Mommie." I would never hit those precious little people whom God had entrusted to my care and who were flesh of my flesh and blood of my blood. I would use love, patience, and understanding.

The entire time that Jerry was in the hospital was very difficult for us. Our television broke and I didn't have the money to have it repaired. It was winter and we were experiencing one of the worst blizzards in fifteen years. We didn't own a radio and the telephone was disconnected because I couldn't pay the bill. The people from the furniture store had come and repossessed the living room furniture and the children's beds. It was Christmas and someone had stolen all the children's Christmas things. But we survived, thank God.

I had hidden the children's Christmas toys and clothes in a closet in a neighbor's apartment who lived down the hall from us. Playing Santa was always a big deal with our family and the Christmas things were stored until Christmas Eve so that I could play Santa for the kids.

Someone broke into the neighbor's apartment and stole everything that Jerry and I had bought, but the thief didn't take anything of Paula's, my neighbor. Furthermore, the thief didn't take Paula's mixer, toaster, stereo, and television, which were all in plain view. Paula had one son and his Christmas toys and clothes were in the front of the closet, and my children's Christmas toys and clothes were in the back of the same closet. The thief would have had to climb over Paula's son's Christmas things to get to ours. They took everything of ours.

To make matters worse, someone broke into our mailbox and stole the check that the welfare agency had sent me as a Santa Claus Anonymous gift. They sent me two dollars per child, which came to a total of eight dollars. Actually, what could I have bought worthwhile for that amount of money?

Welfare was a joke. I went to the Welfare Department for assistance to pay my rent. They gave me the run-around you wouldn't believe. They kept promising to help me, but they never did. Finally, in desperation, I went to a community agency that was housed in the projects to help me get money for rent and groceries.

The woman from the agency came to my apartment to talk with me, and I explained what had happened when I went to the Welfare Department. She called her office and told the director about my situation. She asked if I had enough food to last the night, and said that we would go together the following day to the welfare office, because they were compelled to issue me an emergency check. I told her that we had enough food to last until the following day, but just barely enough. The truth was that I had enough for the children, but not enough for me. I was too embarrassed to tell her that, and too proud to have her feel sorry for me.

Hana and I went to the Welfare Department and put in a claim. Sure enough, they issued me an emergency check and prepared all the papers so that I would receive a regular check each month. I don't see how anyone can spend much time on welfare. I was put through a lot of humiliating changes for that little bit of money. First, the social worker came to visit me and wanted to look through all my clothes closets. When she saw that I had some Italian knit suits and dresses and a suede coat with a mink collar, she told me that I dressed better than she did, and if I expected to receive support for myself and my children from the department, I would have to get rid of my clothes.

In the ghetto, one can buy and find anything and everything "hot." Someone was always selling stolen goods for half the going price. I had bought those clothes hot. However, that didn't matter to her. She could only see that she didn't have clothes as good as mine. She also told me that I was not permitted to have a telephone if I was getting welfare assistance. If I could afford a telephone, then I didn't need the department's help. She also told me that I could not have a man sleep in my apartment with me, not that I wanted anyone to sleep with me. I just didn't like being told I couldn't.

The social worker came often and always unannounced, and each time she checked my clothes closets. I didn't get rid of my clothes as she had instructed me to do, and each time she threatened to discontinue my checks until I complied. I didn't overtly refuse, I just didn't do it, knowing that she never carried out her threats.

I began to wonder whose rules she was quoting, hers or the department's. She began to come very late at night when everyone was asleep, around 2 a.m. or 3 a.m., to see if she could catch a man in my bed. I told her I wasn't going to open my door if she came again at that time of night. She replied that she was just doing her job.

I needed some kitchen chairs, and I asked my social worker if the department could assist me in purchasing them. She looked at my chairs, which were falling apart, and said that I didn't need new ones. The next time she came, I had just waxed the living room floor. We couldn't sit on the living room sofa to talk as we usually did which meant that she had to sit in one of my kitchen chairs. She sat down in the chair and almost fell onto the floor. Had she fallen she might have hurt herself on the concrete floor. I looked at her and smiled. I never said a word. I knew that she knew what I was thinking. Then I said to her, still smiling, "You said that I didn't need new chairs, remember?"

She glared at me and said, "I'll see what I can do," and then she angrily left my apartment.

She returned later in the week and said that the department would be willing to give me five dollars for each chair. Because I needed four chairs, they would give me twenty dollars to buy four kitchen chairs. I angrily replied, "Where in the hell can I buy four chairs for twenty dollars?"

She told me to go to St. Vincent dePaul around the corner. St Vincent dePaul was a place where people donated old, used, unwanted items and clothes. They never had any worthwhile furniture and the clothes they had I wouldn't take as a gift.

I told her that I wanted some decent chairs and any chair sold for five dollars couldn't be much good.

She looked at me with a smirk on her face and said with a sneer, "Why don't you sell some of your clothes and use that money to buy you some kitchen chairs?" Then she turned and walked out the door.

What she didn't know was that I had already bought new kitchen chairs. I had hidden them in the closet and had removed the door knobs so that she couldn't open the closet door. When she saw that the knobs were removed from one closet she accused me of allowing my children to destroy other folks "property."

She said, "People who don't have anything, don't respect what other folks have. I hate to work with colored folks because they don't value anything."

That kind of talk was coming from a black woman. Those are the kind of imprisoned minds that can set the black race back three hundred years. This is what I call, "walking backwards into the future" or "looking at the future through a rearview mirror." However, I let her think what she wanted to think about why the knobs were removed from the closet door. But I told her to get her high-and-mighty self out of my apartment and that if she ever came back again, I would throw her ass off the fourth floor.

I also told her that if my assistance was interrupted in any way, I would personally visit her supervisor. I told her that if she spent every cent she had on clothes she would still look like a dressed-up ape because, short of plastic surgery, nothing could help her, and I doubted very seriously if plastic surgery could do her any good, because if she looked in the mirror at her shape she could see that her messed up body would ruin anything that she put on it.

She left and I immediately called the department and reported her. I told her supervisor that I would go to court before I would let that jealous old battle-ax put her feet on another piece of linoleum that I paid for (I couldn't afford a rug).

After that, I was assigned another worker. I stayed on welfare for about one year. Man, I could not stand going over to the Welfare Department and standing in long lines waiting for food, food stamps, and checks. The only thing that I liked was the cheese they gave us. All the other food reminded me of army rations that Frank often brought home when I was a little girl. I remember saying that I could only eat that stuff if I were dying and that was the only thing that could save me.

After Jerry had been in the hospital for almost a year, I went to the Welfare Department again to try to get assistance to help pay for the hospital bill which had accumulated into the thousands. The welfare people told me that because my husband had been making too much money when he was working, they couldn't help me.

It didn't matter that he was lying in the hospital, fighting for his life, and couldn't take care of himself or his family. It didn't matter that I had four children at home. It didn't matter that Jerry paid taxes when he was working. It didn't matter that we had never used the welfare before. It didn't matter that we were in an emergency situation. It didn't even matter that Jerry had not worked in a year because he had been hospitalized during that time.

The only thing that seemed to matter to the Welfare Department was that when Jerry **was** working, he had made too much money. Obviously, we didn't need the Welfare Department's help when Jerry was working. We needed it while he **was not** working; yet, he had made too much money when he **was** working. I never figured that one out.

I said to the woman at the Welfare Department when she explained that ridiculous policy, "O.K. I am too tired to argue. You cannot get blood out of a turnip. I don't have any money to pay the hospital bill. You'll just have to take my children and me because that's all I have. You can have that ragged furniture in my apartment if you want it. It's in your hands."

Having said that, I went to the hospital administrator the same day, told him what I had done, and said, "The next move is anybody's because the bottom line is, I don't have any money."

Well, I don't know what happened. I don't even know who called whom. I just know that one day I received a call from the hospital telling me that the bill was being taken care of. I didn't ask any questions, because I didn't care who was paying or why. I had said all I could. I was confident that somehow it would work out.

While Jerry was in the hospital, many of the guys who called themselves his friends, were coming around to "help me with my woman needs," as they put it. Why do men think that women just can't wait to have sex with them?

"I know it's been hard for you since your ole' man been in the hospital and can't take care of his duties, so how about letting me help you? I know you must be carrying a load around with you," was the usual line and they actually got angry when I didn't go for it. I sent more husbands home to their wives than I ever thought I'd have to.

Ida lived in one of the low-rise apartments. She and her husband had six children. She was a very attractive small woman and she wore fine clothes. She didn't work outside her home. James, her husband, owned a barbershop in a white section of the city. He wore a suit and tie every day. In fact, I had never seen him without a shirt, a tie, and hat. Ida treated me like trash. She didn't allow her children to play with mine, and, when she passed me on the street, she would turn her head in the opposite direction to avoid speaking to me.

One night while Jerry was in the hospital, there was a knock on my door. I answered it and there was James, Ida's husband. He asked me if he could come inside. When I said yes, he came in, sat at my kitchen table and laid a lot of money on the table in piles of $20, $50 and $100 bills.

He then said, "You are an attractive woman. I have been watching you for years wishing you were mine. I make a lot of money and any or all of this (he was pointing to the money on the table), is yours if you will let me take care of your husband's duties until he comes home, and, who knows, maybe we can build a beautiful relationship that won't stop when he does come home. He sure had his share of women before he was shot and he didn't care who knew it."

"Anyway," he continued, "everyone is saying that either one of your men shot him over you or one of his women shot him, or one of his women's niggers or husbands shot him. But that lie you are telling everyone about Jerry being shot accidentally by a friend at a card game has everybody laughing behind your back, because no one believes that story."

In fact, the story was true. When Jerry was gambling at a friend's house, Willie had just purchased a gun from someone. Neither Jerry nor Willie knew anything about guns. They were examining it and Willie was asking Jerry if he thought the gun was worth what he had paid for it. Not knowing about guns and not knowing that a bullet was in the chamber, Willie pulled the trigger and Jerry fell to the floor.

Willie told Jerry that when his family ate, we would eat also, and he was true to his word. Sometimes he bought groceries for the children and me, and paid our rent. He bought Easter clothes for the children. He paid Jerry's doctor bills, and he gave Jerry money to go to North Carolina after he was released from the hospital to stay with his mother while he was recuperating. We couldn't have foreseen that Jerry didn't heal as the doctors had predicted. His wound became infected and he had to be hospitalized again.

Another funny twist to this story is that all the neighbors knew was that a man was taking care of the kids and me while Jerry was in the hospital. They didn't know about Willie's promise to Jerry. Therefore, the neighbors started spreading the rumor that I was sleeping with the man who shot my husband.

When Jerry's Uncle Jackie couldn't entice me to go to bed with him, he told Jerry the same lie about Willie and me, and Jerry believed it. He would bring it up from time to time in the heat of arguments.

I sat and listened to James and then I said to him, "I don't mind your taking care of my needs while my husband is in the hospital, if your wife and my husband don't mind. Why don't I just ask your wife and see if it's all right with her, and if it is, we can call Jerry and see if he will mind if you spend the night with me tonight? Since you have so many children, I wonder if your wife would mind you giving me a certain amount of money each week. Maybe you can leave it with her and I'll pick it up. Since our relationship will obviously affect her, it's only fair that we include her in the decision-making process. Don't you think so?"

James looked at me as if I had just slapped him, which was exactly what I felt like doing. Then he said in an agitated tone, "Don't be silly. Why would you make a crazy suggestion like that?"

I replied, "It's no crazier than the suggestions you just made. What makes you think that I would even consider someone like you? Chump, why don't you pick up your little chump change and slide out of here before I scream and your wife hears me?" He left, and needless to say, he never spoke to me again. I also told him that if I heard any more rumors about me and my family, I would knock on his door and have a little talk with his wife about his visit and about Nora, who lived on the third floor, under me. His eyes got as big as saucers when I mentioned Nora. Obviously, he didn't know that I knew he had been having an affair with her for almost a year.

Nora was a single parent whose apartment was right by the stairs. James always sneaked up and down the stairs to visit her. I didn't know Nora, but I knew someone who did, someone whom Nora visited regularly. There were no secrets in the projects if you had buddies living there, because everyone talked about everybody's business.

I sat in the bar across the street from the projects one day and watched one girlfriend keep the wife occupied and engaged in conversation while the other girlfriend went upstairs to have sex with the husband. Man, oh, man, sometimes the women in the projects were treacherous.

When Jerry was released from the hospital, the bed sores on his buttocks had healed. He had developed bed sores because he was left lying in the same position for long periods in the hospital. He had lost a lot of weight. However, the doctors were very optimistic about his recovery. He decided that he wanted to go to North Carolina to visit his family.

He wanted to stay there until he regained his weight and strength, and I agreed with him. We figured that the separation would give us time to decide what we were going to do about our marriage. We had been pulling in different directions for so long that I had gotten accustomed to being without him. At least we didn't have our famous weekly fights. Before he was shot, we fought every Thursday, Friday, and Saturday night. We fought mostly about me going out. He wanted to go out and play but he wouldn't stand for my going out.

Before Jerry left for North Carolina, my sister and her husband came to visit us from Boston, Massachusetts. We were all sitting in the bedroom talking one morning, when Jerry began complaining of pains in his stomach. He had been home from the hospital for only three weeks, so naturally, we thought it must be the healing process that was causing his discomfort. The pains kept getting more severe.

Sandy, her husband and I took Jerry back to the hospital. They rushed him into the emergency room. As soon as the doctor removed the bandages from Jerry's wound, a foul smelling substance squirted from it. The wound had become infected. Jerry was readmitted to the hospital and stayed for another two months.

When he was released the second time, he began making plans again to leave for North Carolina. We decided that he would take the girls with him and that I would go to Boston to visit my sister and take Butchie with me, because he was the youngest. Butchie was three years old at the time.

I stayed in Boston about three months. While I was there, I received a letter from Jerry's uncle telling me that Jerry was back in the hospital and the girls were staying with someone in the projects and had been there for about a week. I immediately returned to Baltimore.

Butchie and I arrived on a Greyhound bus at about 6 a.m. one Friday morning. The streets were deserted. I had forgotten how dull and boring Baltimore really was. After spending time in Boston, I didn't know whether I wanted to stay in Baltimore anymore. The entire time in Boston I worried about our apartment in Baltimore. I always expected to receive a letter or call from someone informing me that someone had broken into our apartment and cleaned us out. Butchie and I arrived home safely and to my surprise, and relief, everything was just as I had left it. I went to bed intending to get up later in the day and go to visit Jerry in the hospital.

At about 7:30 a.m. there was a knock on the door. I couldn't imagine who would be knocking on my door that early in the morning, especially because no one knew that I had returned to Baltimore. I opened the door and there stood Jericka smiling. Her whole face lit up when she saw me. I bent down, hugged her, and said, "Hi Baby, how did you know that Mommie had come home?"

She hugged me as tight as her little arms would allow her. She kept jumping up and down with glee as she hugged me and she answered, "I didn't know. Everybody said that you had run away and left us and that you were never coming back. But I didn't believe them. I knew that you would come back some day. Everyday I came up here and knocked on the door and I knew that one day you were going to be home and open the door." I cried and hugged my precious little daughter and I promised myself and my daughter right then and there that I would never leave my children again, and I never did.

I can imagine what Jericka must have been feeling; coming every day, knocking on the door of an empty apartment that she and her family called "home," hoping that someday the door would open and she would look up to see her mother, yet leaving every day in disappointment when the door remained closed.

It must have hurt to listen to the children in the projects repeating what they heard the grownups say, that I had run off and left my children. I can imagine how my kids must have cried themselves to sleep each night wondering, "Maybe it's true, maybe our mother did leave us. Maybe she won't come back." I think that as long as the apartment stayed empty, they had hope that I would return, but if someone had moved into it, they might have stopped hoping. Thank God they didn't give up hope.

I went to visit Jerry's uncle to find out what put Jerry back into the hospital. He told me that Jerry had taken a job in North Carolina before he was completely healed. He was working in a chemical plant and chemicals had gotten into the wound and caused internal problems. Then his uncle began talking about how he wanted to go to bed with me. I told him that I was surprised because he was Jerry's uncle.

He said, "Hell, my nephew don't give a damn. He used my place plenty of times with his women. He sometimes brings two with him, one for me and one for him. At least we're keeping it in the family. I know you got to be doing something with somebody since Jerry been hurt and it might as well be me."

Then he put his hand on my thigh and began rubbing it. I removed his hand and told him not to touch me again. He just laughed and put his hand right back on my thigh. That time I used more force to remove his hand, and told him that I would tell Jerry if he did it again and I knew that Jerry would kill him when he came home.

He just grinned and said, "You can tell that red nigga anything you want to and he'll believe his unk. He'll believe me before he'll believe you. We blood. You're the outsider."

That was the way I felt when I was around Jerry's family. I was always the outsider. I didn't belong and Jerry didn't make me feel wanted when his family was around. No matter what I did or said, I was always wrong. I was an outsider in my own family, because I was the stepchild. I was the outsider with my real father's family, because I was illegitimate. I was an outsider with my husband's family, because I was his second wife. I just didn't feel I had a place anywhere.

I think that was one of my driving forces, one of the things that drove me to achieve, to succeed. I felt that I had to keep proving over and over to myself that, "I am somebody." I had allowed so many people to make me feel left out and not wanted. Feeling the pains of rejection, I thought I had to fill my life with things that people could approve of and maybe then they would be proud of me and I would no longer be the outsider.

Jerry had lost so much weight. He had gone from 180 pounds to 98 pounds. He was just skin and bones. The doctors didn't expect him to live, because he kept having so many complications. They couldn't get him to gain any weight. They kept giving him vitamins and trying out new medications, but nothing worked. They even had a thick, white liquid that looked like a vanilla milkshake flown in from Korea. They fed that to him constantly, trying to get him to gain weight, but it didn't work, either. Then one day the doctor told me that there was nothing more they could do for my husband. He was now in the hands of God.

Jerry was so frail and weak that we had to pin his clothes on him and then tie them. I told the doctor, "Just let me take him home. I'll make him gain weight." They told me five years ago that I would lose my twins because they were premature and the doctors couldn't get them to gain weight. I told the doctors that if they could get them strong enough to come home, I would do the rest.

When Jerry came home, I started feeding him collard greens, and taking the juice (the pot liquor) and mashing corn bread up in it, then feeding that to Jerry. When I brought him back to the hospital for a check-up three weeks later, the nurse cried when she saw him. She couldn't believe it was the same person. Jerry had gained weight and was walking straight instead of bent over the way he had been when he left the hospital. The doctor praised me and said that my "pot liquor" should be in the medical journal. He was joking, of course, but Jerry improved and never went back to the hospital for that gunshot wound again.

Concrete City

Believe it or not, moving into the projects was a step up from our third floor walk-up on Lafayette Avenue. We moved into the projects after the triplets were born. There was a long waiting list for the projects, but we were moved up because we had the triplets. Our one bedroom apartment was too small. The triplets were premature and very sickly. The visiting nurse told us they needed to sleep alone for health reasons. That was why we were given priority getting into the projects.

We moved from Lafayette Avenue right after a white man had chased me one night when I was pregnant with the triplets as I was returning from the hospital clinic. Jericka was about three months old and had developed a diaper rash, so I had taken her to the clinic for treatment. We had been in the hospital all day waiting to be seen by a doctor and now it was pushing dark.

As we turned onto my street, I saw a white man standing on the opposite corner. I started running, and so did he. I tried to pick up both

Jericka and the stroller but they were too heavy so I took her out of the stroller and ran up the steps to my apartment building. I couldn't find my keys, so I started screaming and kicking on the door. Luckily, the man who lived on the first floor was coming out of his apartment, heard my screams, and opened the door. When the white man saw my neighbor coming to the door, he ran.

When we moved I thought, at last I can go outside, meet neighbors and not be so lonely. But life in the projects would prove to be hell.

In the Baltimore projects, you knew you were poor because everyone around you was either on welfare, hustling, or working a little jive job for low pay. I was luckier than most, because I had a husband who worked. That is one good thing I could always say about Jerry, he worked and he wasn't lazy. Even when he came home so drunk he couldn't stand up, he would sleep and get up for work the next day. Sure he complained about hangovers, headaches, upset stomachs, and being sick, but he still went, and not late, either. He was always at work at least a half-hour early.

I have never figured out how mice could get into an apartment with concrete floors and walls on the fourth floor of a high-rise project. Once I went into the bathroom and saw a baby mouse swimming around in the commode trying to get out. I searched for a mouse hole, but couldn't find one. I flushed the mouse away.

Another day I was washing my hands when I heard a little splash. I looked in the direction of the noise and saw a mouse in the stool. It must have fallen from somewhere, although the ceiling was concrete, too. Later I learned that they came in by crawling between the floors along the pipes. That seemed odd, because the apartments had steam heat. You could hear the steam when it came on because the pipes made a popping noise.

The project manager turned on the heat at a specified time in the fall, turned it off the same way in the spring. No matter if the weather outside was zero, on a certain date, the heat was turned off. Conversely, it didn't matter if it was 100 degrees outside, on a specified date, the heat was turned on. The schedule was kept regardless of how absurd it was. Sometimes it got so hot in the apartment, we couldn't stand it. It seemed the comfort of the tenants didn't matter to management.

And was it ever noisy. Anyone who ever lived in the projects must remember the street corner singing. Our apartment was right above the playground. Every night teenagers gathered there and sang. They had some beautiful voices too. They sang all the most popular tunes recorded by the current top artists, such as Little Melvin and the Blue Notes, the Four Tops, Sam and Dave, and Smokey Robinson and the Miracles. They were usually male singing groups. Very seldom did females sing outside unless they were backing up a male group. Boy, could they harmonize. I would lie sweltering in the heat, listening to the brothers sing.

One night I saw Jerry walking across the playground with another woman. I watched them enter the elevator of the building across the street from ours. Although I could not see inside the elevator, each floor had what we called an elevator waiting area. A person could stand across the street from the building and see people getting on and off the elevator. I could see all the floors through the elevator waiting area's window. When the elevator stopped, I saw Jerry and the woman get off together and walk to her apartment. I counted the floors and determined that it was the sixth floor. I put on a jacket and walked over there.

On the way I met a policeman walking his beat. I told him, "I think you had better go with me. I just saw my husband go into an apartment with another woman and I'm going up there to knock on the door. If he doesn't come out, I'm going to wait for him. There is only one way out. He has to pass me and when he does, I will kill him." I showed the policeman the butcher knife I had under my jacket.

He said, "Lady, you're going to get in trouble with that knife. Why don't you go on back home?"

I said, "I'm not going to let him play under my nose. He won't embarrass me like this. If he wants to play he can go across town, but I will not accept being laughed at on my own turf."

The policeman said, "I see your point. I'll go with you to keep you out of trouble."

We went to the sixth floor and knocked on the woman's apartment door. A nice-looking female about my age answered the door. I asked for Jerry. She denied knowing him.

I told the officer, "I know what I saw, and I am not leaving."

The officer asked the woman if we could enter and she said we could. I walked in first and turned on the light in the frontroom. Her apartment was laid out exactly like ours. Just then the telephone rang and she answered it. Apparently it was one of her friends asking if something was wrong, because I heard her say, "Nothing, this girl thinks her husband is in my house. I don't even know who she is talking about."

Just then I heard the policeman say, "Come on out from under there." I walked in the direction of the voice, and saw the officer in the woman's bedroom shining his flashlight under her bed. Jerry came crawling out looking embarrassed and guilty.

The policeman said to him, "Why don't you go home to your family?" What made me so angry was that Jerry was wearing my new white sweater under the woman's bed. He and I argued all the way home, and once we got there, we fought half the night. The noise woke the children.

Our apartment was next to the garbage shoot. The shoot went to the incinerator in the basement. Every day garbage got stuck inside the shoot and the smoke filled our apartment. That meant that we had to vacate the apartment until the smoke cleared. We often woke up in the middle of the night unable to breathe because the apartment was filled with smoke from the incinerator.

Jerry worked in a children's clothing store and he often brought the kids clothes that were samples. The salesmen liked Jerry and they always brought things from New York for our children. One Easter a salesman gave Jerry beautiful lace dresses for our girls. Jericka dripped some chocolate ice cream on hers and I washed it and hung it to dry in a locked bin in the basement.

There were washing machines and dryers in the basement of each building. There were individual bins where tenants could string their own clotheslines, hang their clothes to dry, and padlock the doors to secure their laundry. The only way into the bins other than through the door was to climb over the fence separating each bin. When I went to get Jericka's dress, someone had climbed over the fence, torn the dress into shreds, and hung the pieces back on the line. I cried because someone could be that cruel. I would have felt better if the dress had been stolen.

Because the playground was concrete, the entire apartment was concrete, and it was a city within a city, we called the projects, "Concrete City." When we first moved into the projects, the playground was a beautiful grassy area. The elevator room was heated and secured with doors. People mopped each tier, washed their windows, and even washed the outer walls of their apartments.

They also scrubbed the stairs. The residents at that time were racially mixed. Elderly white and young white families lived there. The family next door to Gladys had a white school teacher and the family next door to them was an older white couple who were both retired. The family in the corner apartment was an older white woman with a young son who cursed her out, would fight her, and one day he set the elevator on fire. He said he was trying to burn her up.

On the other side of me was a young white family who didn't like "colored" people, as they said. Because we lived so close, it was inevitable that our children would play together. They had small children and so did I. The children never had a problem playing together.

It was the adults who couldn't get along with each other. When Jericka was about five years old, she was riding her tricycle on the ramp when the little boy, who was about six, hit her and took her tricycle. After Jericka ran into the house crying, I knocked on the door of the adjacent apartment to talk to the little boy's mother. A tall, stocky white male answered the door and started calling me names and said that I should keep my daughter in the house. When I told Jerry what the man said, Jerry went to see him. When Jerry knocked on the door, the man opened it and then three other white men tried to pull Jerry inside.

I ran to help him and started screaming for the neighbors to call the police. One of the men down the ramp heard my screams and ran to help us. We looked as if we were playing tug-of-war, with the three men trying to pull Jerry into their apartment while a neighbor and me were trying to pull him out. Who knows what they would have done to Jerry had they succeeded in getting him inside.

The police came and put Jerry and me in the police van. (We called the vans "black mariah" because they were all black. They aren't used anymore.) They took us to jail and locked up Jerry for disturbing the peace, although he was the one with the bruises and black eye. When we explained to the officer on duty what happened, he let Jerry go. We immediately swore out a warrant on the man.

However, when we returned home they were gone. Sometime in the night, they had moved. For about a month the police couldn't find the man to serve the warrant.

Then, one day when I was on Lombard Street (called "Corn Beef Row" because you could buy the best corned beef in town there), I saw the big white man who had initiated the attack. When he saw me, he started calling me names and laughing about how he had beaten up my husband and how his son had slapped my little nigger daughter. I just ignored him and he soon walked away, but I followed him.

When I saw where he had gone, I called the police from a telephone booth. When they came, I told them that a warrant was out for a man who was in the apartment I pointed out. The police asked how I knew about the warrant and I told them that I had sworn it out. When the police locked him up, he wasn't laughing anymore. We went to trial and the man was fined.

As more Blacks moved into the projects, more white families moved out, until they were occupied by Blacks only. The projects became a place where you could buy anything, including death. For twelve years Jerry and I lived there with our children. We watched it change over the years and we watched the buildings around the projects change.

We lived in the projects during the riots. The cleaners on the corner had some of my clothes in it and they were lost when the building that housed the cleaners was burned during the riots. There was a bar across the street from the building where I lived that didn't allow Blacks to come inside. It was destroyed completely and its contents were scattered in the streets.

Yet, the bar next door, which was owned by a white former police officer and catered to Black neighbors wasn't touched. The neighbors had hung a black cloth on the door of that bar as a symbol that it was to be spared. That was the way stores in the black neighborhoods were treated. If a black cloth was on the door, that business was not touched, because its owners were O.K.

But we destroyed our own neighborhoods during the riots. We weren't hurting anyone but ourselves. When my baby's milk was gone, I couldn't find a store open in my neighborhood where I could buy milk. They were all destroyed. They were either burned out or all the contents had been looted. Those with black cloths on the doors had been closed out of fear. The owners were scared to open. That was a part of the riots I could not understand. We were hurting ourselves because, when it was all over, we had to go into white neighborhoods to shop.

We had completely destroyed our own neighborhoods, but we didn't go into the white neighborhoods and destroy their property. Now we had to go there and give them our money, because that's where the food stores were after everything was all over. I still wonder, what did we accomplish?

Stores that once had eye-appealing window displays put up iron bars and steel covers on their windows. Friendliness between customers and store owners was gone as owners put bullet-proof partitions between customers and clerk. What did the riots accomplish? It seems to me we lost more than we gained. The slogan, "Burn, Baby, Burn," was chanted in every black inner-city neighborhood. "Black Power" and "Soul Brother," "Sister Lady" and "Brother Man," were identity exchanges between Blacks, while white armed soldiers of the national guard drove through our neighborhoods with signs on their jeeps that read, "Sorry, We're all Souled Out." Again, I ask, what did we accomplish?

The Rape

Funny, then again, maybe it's not funny, but I haven't thought about that awful night in years. I'm glad, though. Maybe I'll stop blaming myself for what happened to Martha Belle. It also makes me suspicious of so-called "male friends" who volunteer to "do me a favor."

I remember the incident as if it were yesterday, and for me, it will always be yesterday, today, and tomorrow, because Martha Belle ("Marty") will never be here to see her children become adults. She will never see her grandchildren, and her grandchildren will be deprived forever of the wisdom and the love of their grandmother.

Marty's son was cheated of the chance to know his mother, and he is left with the terrible scar of seeing his mother killed. I know that it could be said that she has gone to a better place, that she has no more worries, no more fears, and all of that may be true if she knew God.

But try telling that to a little boy who cries himself to sleep every night calling for his mommie, who will never answer. Try telling that to Marty's mother when she looks at her daughter's picture and knows that she cannot telephone and hear her daughter's voice. Try telling that to a little boy who still has nightmares about his mother's death.

It was Saturday night after the bars and nightclubs had closed. We were at Joanie's and Jimmy's house. The entire crowd always went up to Joanie's and Jimmy's on weekends. It was understood that's where we would go. No one asked, "Where are you going later on? Where is the party?" We just bought some liquor and sodas before the bars closed. Those of us who didn't have cars made arrangements to ride with someone who did, because we knew that everyone was going to the same place.

Joanie and Jimmy were close friends of ours. We all thought of them as the all-time perfect couple. They were such a twosome that they seemed more like brother and sister than husband and wife. I always envied them; I wanted my marriage to be just like theirs. That is, I did in my younger life when Jerry and I were going our separate ways and Joanie was always with her husband.

However, years later, I thank God that Jerry was the husband he was. They once seemed like the ideal couple, but, as the years went by, things changed. Once they did everything together; they got high together; they went on trips together. They always acted as if they were so much in love. After twenty years, they were still hugging and kissing like newlyweds. It was a pleasure to be around them.

There was no need for an invitation to Joanie and Jimmy's house. You knew where to find everyone in our crowd or anyone who was part of the crowd that hung out at Lee's Bar, Bernie's Cocktail Lounge, or any of the nightclubs on Myrtle Avenue, Saratoga Street, Fayette Street, Pine and Vine Streets, Freemount Avenue, or Baltimore Street. That was our territory. We never hung on The Avenue. That was the "big time" night life. Although we hung out in the streets, we never forgot that we had children to take care of. Joanie had six children and I had four.

Everyone down in our territory knew Joanie and me. We were always together. Whenever you saw me, you saw Joanie and when you saw Joanie, you knew that I wasn't far behind. When we moved to opposite sides of town, we still met at Bernie's Cocktail Lounge.

We got high at Bernie's every weekend, starting on Thursday and ending on Sunday, smoking marijuana; drinking Robitussin AC cough syrup because it contained codeine; popping uppers and downers; taking speed; drinking Colt 45 Malt Liquor, Canadian Club, and Squirt. Man, when I think about those days, I don't know how we survived. We had babies at home and we were hanging out in the streets with people who had no responsibilities or at least were not concerned about those responsibilities. Anyway, they didn't show concern.

I was going to Morgan State at the time. When classes were over, instead of going home, I would go directly down to Bernie's, put my books behind the bar, and hang out with the crowd. I had just left my college friends and now I was hanging with my "street friends." It was funny that I was accepted by both sets of "friends," and I felt comfortable socializing with both.

However, with the crowd at Bernie's, I felt that was where I belonged. Because of my childhood and because I was living in the projects, surrounded by that type of crowd every day, I felt that was my life.

I felt uncomfortable with the kids from college, because their parents were professionals, such as teachers, or social workers, or members of other professions. Thank God I realized that I could make a difference in my life while I still had a chance to make a difference.

The syrup house on the corner of Pine and Mulberry Streets was where I spent both a lot of my time and my money. At that time, you could buy four ounces of Robitussin syrup at a drug store for $1.25. Then it went up to $1.75. After a while, the sale of the syrup without a prescription was banned, especially after it was obvious that so many people were becoming addicted to it. That's when people like "Big Dan" began operating "syrup houses" and the people in my crowd started hanging out there.

We sat warming the syrup on the old potbellied stove that stood in the center of the front room of the house. Candles were used to light most of the rooms in the house. The operators only wanted the house for syrup, not as a residence. They didn't need to use the upstairs. Some folks used it to smoke reefer or to do other things. We would drink the warm syrup, then take either three "yellow jackets," or two "big reds," (downers). They are sleeping capsules normally given to hospital patients to relax them for sleep.

The yellow capsules or "yellow jackets" were smaller than the "big reds," and less potent. We could buy yellow jackets three for a quarter and big reds, two for a quarter. Then we would drink a Colt 45 and nod all night. The syrup made you itch so you would scratch and nod like a junkie. Also, syrup could be addictive if it was consumed on a regular basis.

Foolish as we were, we also took pills called Robin Eggs, Quaaludes, Christmas Trees, Black Beauties, Purple Haze, and Sunshine (speed). We smoked Angel Dust and marijuana. We didn't try heroin; we were afraid of needles, and I saw the way that people who were shooting looked as they nodded and scratched. We didn't snort cocaine because we couldn't afford it, and we were afraid of becoming addicted to it.

After I met Joanie and her crowd and they accepted me, I felt that I had some "friends" who wanted me. Now that I think back to those years, I can see that I was lying to myself. My street crowd called me "Dumb Barbara, Stupid Barbara" and said that I graduated from "Dumb High," because I wasn't street smart as they were. They laughed at the way I dressed when I first met them.

I wore my dresses long, no makeup, and my hair was pulled back into a bun at the back of my neck. They made fun of the way I talked, because I had a southern accent. Joanie said that when she first met me, I only wanted to talk about children, cooking, and housework. Well, that was all I knew. Joanie started paying a babysitter so that I could go out. I wanted to please the crowd because I wanted to be one of them.

The gang, especially Joanie, were training me. Every time I tried to drink, I would get sick and vomit. For two days afterward, I couldn't keep anything in my stomach. I tried eating greasy foods to "put a lining on my stomach," as the gang said. That didn't work. I took Alka Seltzer before I started drinking and after I stopped. I still got sick. Joanie said it was because I always drank something sweet with my alcohol; but I couldn't drink it any other way. I had to have something to mask the taste.

Sometimes my "friends" left me sitting at the bar waiting for them. They would tell me they would be right back, so I would sit and wait. Often, they never came back. I guess I really didn't fit in there either. I always had to play down my education. Sometimes, I had to act dumb about certain subjects.

Frequently when we were talking, someone would make a remark such as, "You are letting that little education go to your head." I might say something as inconsequential as, "The rain is really coming down hard," and someone would make an issue of it, saying something like, "Oh, you think you know everything because you go to college. We got eyes. We know it's raining." I often remained silent so that they wouldn't accuse me of "showing off." I guess that's why I indulged in a lot of things; I was trying to fit in.

One night we were in Lee's Bar sitting around talking, joking, telling lies, and having what we called a good time. We never did any harm or started fights, or got loud and embarrassed ourselves. We decided that we wanted to go for a ride. The only person who had a car was Donnie and because he was one of us, we knew it would be all right.

Donnie was a quiet light-skinned, skinny man with red hair, in his late twenties or early thirties. He was neither good-looking, nor ugly. He was just a "red man," and in the 1960s if you were light-skinned, you were automatically thought to be good-looking. Light was almost white, and white was what everyone wanted to be like. We all piled into Donnie's car and went riding. We didn't have a particular destination in mind; we were just high on reefer and wanted to ride.

No sooner had we reached the highway, Donnie began driving like a crazy man, swerving across the highway, driving awfully fast, as if he were racing with someone. We kept yelling for him to slow down, but the more we hollered, the faster he drove. I was very frightened. I thought he was crazy and we all would be killed.

Finally, we reached Joanie's house. When I stepped from the car, I was trembling. Everyone laughed at me and called me "chicken," but I knew they were just as frightened as I was. They just didn't want to admit it. I didn't want to be different from the crowd so I just laughed it off.

After we had smoked a couple of joints, we got back into Donnie's car and started back downtown to Bernie's. This time, I couldn't keep quiet; I didn't care if they did call me chicken; I was scared. I started shouting at Donnie either to slow down or to stop the car so I could get out. Everyone else began to shout the same thing.

Abruptly, he pulled the car over to the side of the road by Hilton Park, in an area that was very dark and isolated. We were more afraid of being left alone in the dark than we were of Donnie's driving. He said, "O.K., dammit. Get the fuck out." He turned around and gave me a menacing look.

I replied in a trembling voice, "Ain't no way I am going to get out in this dark park and I don't want to ride with no fool either. I just want you to get me back safely where you got me from and I promise that you won't ever have to worry about me getting into your car again."

Donnie replied, "Well, just shut-the-fuck-up and let me drive my damn car the way I want to."

I was afraid of him but I couldn't let my fear show, so I said, trying to act tough, "You won't drive this car like a crazy man as long as I am in here. My life is at stake just like everybody else's." We argued back and forth until we reached Bernie's. By that time, everyone in the car was thoroughly disgusted and angry with him, but he didn't seem to care what anyone thought.

Donnie and I were in each other's company a couple of times after that incident, but I never got into his car after that night. Every time someone suggested that we go for a ride with Donnie, I refused. Almost every time we were at Joanie's house, Donnie was there. He would come in, stay a few minutes and then leave. It was as if he really didn't fit in now.

He apologized for acting so crazy that night and for using profanity to me. He said he had too much to drink and asked if I would please forgive him and he promised that it would never happen again. He said that he liked and respected everyone in the crowd and he just wanted to be our friend.

I felt sorry for him and said, "Of course, I will forgive you. We all had too much to drink that night. We all act like fools at times and that was your night to act like a fool, and it was your car. I had no business getting into it if I didn't like the way you were driving."

We both laughed and he extended his hand and said, "Shake on it, friend," and we did.

About two months after we had agreed to forgive and forget, we were at Joanie's house on a Saturday night. I don't know where Jerry was, we were seldom together on the weekends. He did his thing with his crowd, which didn't include me, and I did likewise with my crowd, trying desperately not to think what he was doing and with whom.

Anyway, that Saturday night we were all at Joanie's having a party, drinking, smoking, and having a good time. About 2 a.m., I started to get ready to leave. Joanie asked me why I was leaving so early. I said that I wanted to leave before the last bus left "the Junction," so I wouldn't be stuck without transportation home.

Taxi fare would have been too expensive. Joanie said that she would ask Donnie if he would drop me off at home, because he was taking some other people home in the same area. I agreed on condition that he wouldn't drive like a maniac. Donnie overheard me and he laughed and said he promised to drive "sensibly." I agreed to ride with him and we continued to have a good time a little longer now that I had transportation home.

The other riders were three lady friends of Joanie's. They weren't a part of our regular crowd and they were a few years older than we were. We all got into Donnie's car and we chatted along the way about nothing in particular.

Because they lived on one side of Fayette Street and I lived on the side where Donnie lived, he decided to take them home first. I remarked that he should be a cab driver, because he knew all the shortcuts to Bond Street. I wasn't afraid of Donnie that night. He wasn't driving fast. He was taking part in the conversation, laughing and joking with all of us just like one of the crowd.

After he dropped the others off, he started driving in the direction of the projects. When he had come within a block of my building, he pulled the car to the side of the street in front of Dave's Bar and turned the motor off. I thought that he was going to light a joint to smoke before he took me home, so I didn't think there was cause for alarm. I thought when he reached into his glove compartment, he was looking for his reefer, but instead he pulled out a gun and demanded that I undress.

I thought it was a joke and said, "O.K. O.K., cowboy, I know you're bad. Now put that thing away, cut out the bullshit and roll a joint." I was laughing because I thought he was just showing me his gun. It wasn't unusual for anyone in the crowd to carry a gun. We hung out in some pretty rough bars sometimes, and protection didn't hurt.

Donnie cocked the trigger and said in a menacing voice I had heard before, "If you think I am playing, I'll just shoot it to let you know that it's loaded and that I mean business. Now take that damn shit off before I tear it off of you and hurt you real bad." I had never seen him like that. I tried to talk to him calmly. I tried to keep my voice from shaking, but I wasn't carrying it off.

I said, "Donnie, you don't really mean this. We're friends. Why would you want to do this? You have been to my house, and met my husband, and partied with us. Remember the night we all came to my apartment when Joanie's house was being painted? Why would you want to hurt me now?"

Donnie wasn't buying it. He replied, "You are a very good-looking woman and you have the sexiest walk that I have ever seen. I used to just sit and watch you walk, but you never noticed me. I was only someone to laugh at. I watched you flirt with other guys, and I said that someday you would look my way, but you never did. I don't give a damn about those other motherfuckers in that crowd, I just wanted to be around you. You don't know how many wet dreams I have had just dreaming about you and the way you walk. A woman like you shouldn't be allowed to live."

When he said that, I really got scared. I began pleading with him. Then he put the gun to my head and demanded that I undress. I hoped that Jean, my friend who lived on the second floor of my building, was at home. I thought that if I could get Donnie to go to Jean's apartment with me, maybe I could get help.

Jean had three big sons, and it was possible that she had male company. She was separated from her husband and lived alone with her three sons and one daughter.

I said to Donnie, "Look, I want you just as much as you want me, but I thought you were too sophisticated for me. Why should you ruin a beautiful night trying to make love in this small car? Why don't we go to my girlfriend's apartment so that we can both enjoy it?"

He paused for a moment and I thought he was going for it, but then he said, "Naw, I don't trust you. You'll get to your friend's house and then you'll have help, and I won't get anything. Do you think I'm stupid? Take off your fucking clothes and I ain't telling you no mo. I swear I'll shoot this motherfucker. I ought to shoot it anyway just so you can hear the sound of it."

I knew that Jerry hung out at Dave's Bar, and I also knew that he had been messing around with a woman that lived in the projects across the street from Dave's. If Jerry was over there now he would have to walk past where we were parked to get home.

I said to Donnie, "Suppose my husband passes by here? I can't take my clothes off here. He passes this way all the time."

Donnie answered, "You better hope that he don't pass by here and see us cause if he do, he's a dead man, and if you tell him about this and he comes in my face and say something 'bout it, I'll kill him." Now, I knew he was for real, so I started to take off my clothes.

I took off my clothes from the waist down and I was sitting in the car half naked. I again tried to talk him in to going to Jean's apartment, but he wouldn't. Instead, he started the motor with his left hand while he kept the gun to my head with his right hand. We drove up Baltimore Street, which was just before my street. I was afraid that if I tried anything, the gun would go off, whether accidentally or deliberately, and I had decided that it was not worth dying for pride.

We drove for a few minutes until he found a secluded spot behind some projects. He stopped the car, ordered me into the back seat, and climbed in behind me. He unzipped his pants and started to put his penis inside me, but just as his penis touched my vagina, he ejaculated.

After it was over, Donnie began apologizing, saying how sorry he was. He begged me not to tell anyone and not to hate him. Then, just as quickly, his mood changed. He flew into a rage and said if I told my husband, he would kill him. He said, "If you love your ol' man and you want your children to have a father, you better let this be our secret, cause I'll kill him, so help me, if he ever mentions it to me." I believed him. Then he dropped me off in front of my building and apologized again.

I went into the house and filled the bathtub with water as hot as I could stand, got in, and sat soaking. I scrubbed my skin so hard it began to burn. I could still smell him in my skin, and the smell made me sick to my stomach. Jerry wasn't home, only Gayle, my babysitter. Jerry didn't come home that night and I wanted to so much to be held and comforted.

I ran downstairs to Jean's apartment, woke her, and told her what happened. I asked her what I should do. I was afraid if I called the police, they would embarrass me with all kinds of questions, and if Jerry found out about it, Donnie would kill him, because Donnie was crazy. Jean said, "If I were you, I'd just chalk it up to experience and forget about it."

I took her advice and didn't mention it to anyone. Each time I saw Donnie after that night, I would turn my head and not speak to him.

He walked up to me one night at Bernie's and said, "Are you going to make me pay for one mistake for the rest of my life? Why can't you forgive me and speak to me again?"

I looked at him and said, "Because you are pathetic. If you ever come near me again, I will kill you. I bought me something to protect myself against animals like you and I will not hesitate to use it. No one will ever treat me that way again, making me drive up a damn street half-naked and forcing me to do what I don't want to do, and then have the nerve to threaten my family. Who in-the- fuck do you think you are? Do you think you are the only one who can carry a gun? If you ever go near my husband, you crazy motherfucker, I'll blow your balls off."

The truth was, I didn't have anything. I was deathly afraid of guns, and I was afraid to use a knife. I was just bluffing so that he would not try that again. It worked, because he didn't know if I was bluffing or not.

Months later, I told Joanie about the rape and found out that he had done the same thing to Justine, Joanie's sister. It was almost the same pattern, but he had offered her twenty-five dollars not to tell. She didn't take the money, but she was too ashamed to tell anyone except her sister about the rape.

About six months later, I was reading the newspaper and I saw that Martha Bell Slaughter ("Marty") had been murdered by her husband while their three year old son sat in the car and watched. I didn't make the connection right away because I didn't know Donnie's last name. Then Joanie called saying, "Guess what, Donnie just killed his wife." Marty was Joanie's cousin.

It appeared that Marty had been going out with her girlfriends and Donnie didn't like it. He was very jealous and falsely accused her of fooling around with another man. On several occasions, he had followed her to the store, and to her mother's house, spying on her. He often beat her if he came home and she wasn't there.

This day, he and his young son Mike, were at home sleeping. When Donnie woke up and found that Marty was gone, he flew into a rage, grabbed a shotgun, put their son in the car, and took off driving like crazy, looking for Marty. Donnie went to Marty's mother's house and everywhere else he thought she might be, but he couldn't find her. By this time he was crazy with anger and blind with jealousy.

Finally, on the way home he rode past a dry cleaners shop and saw Marty standing inside talking to the clerk, who was a male. Donnie left his son in the car and walked over to look through the window, making sure it was Marty. When he was certain, he ran back to the car, picked up the shotgun, and fired it through the window, killing Marty instantly. The blast blew away one side of her face. Donnie fired again at the clerk, but he ducked behind the counter out of the line of fire.

The sad thing is that his wife was there getting Marty's dry cleaning. The clerk's wife could not be seen through the window, because she was standing behind a rack of clothes searching for Marty's order. Marty had been talking to the wife, not the man; he was there working on receipts from the register. Marty's son sat in the car and witnessed the entire thing.

After Donnie shot his wife, he calmly got back into the car, sat his son in his lap, and waited for the police. Donnie is now serving time for the murder, but I often wonder if things would have been different if we had told the police and our husbands about Donnie. Could it have saved Marty's life? We'll never know.

I was almost raped by different men three other times when I lived in the projects. Anything could happen there. I was attending The Johns Hopkins University at night. After classes I had to catch buses most of the time because Jerry always said he had something else to do.

One night when I was coming home from class, I noticed a man standing outside the projects, leaning on the wire fence that separated the sidewalk from the yards of the people who lived on the ground level floor. The projects had twelve floors, and the man was looking up at the building as if waiting for someone.

Just as I approached him, he turned and began to walk toward me. When he was close enough to touch me, he grabbed me around the waist with his right hand, and began feeling my vagina with his left. I screamed, swung around to loosen his grip, and began to run. He ran after me. I ran to the elevator and I was lucky because an empty elevator was waiting there. I jumped on it and frantically pushed the button to close the door. It closed just as he reached it. I made it to the fourth floor, and into my apartment safely. As usual, Jerry was not at home. Only the babysitter was there, and she was asleep.

After I calmed down and began to think about what had just happened, I got really scared as I realized what could have happened.

First, it was not a good idea for me to get in the elevator, because if the man had just been a few seconds quicker, he would have reached the elevator before the doors closed and I would have been trapped in there with him. He could have stopped it between the floors, raped me, and no one would have come to my rescue.

Even if I had screamed, it was unlikely that I would have been heard because the noise in the projects at night with eighty-four poor black families crowded into one building was very loud. Besides, had my screams been heard, it wouldn't have helped.

Kids were always playing around, screaming in the elevators. Why would anyone tell my screams as a sign of trouble? Even if they did, nobody would want to get involved. Oh sure, the bell in the elevator would ring if the elevator stopped between floors, but project residents had long since stopped paying attention to it. It happened too often.

Teenagers would stop the elevators between the floors to neck. The bell ringing had become a regular occurrence. After that horrible night, I became more cautious when I came home alone.

Another time I was almost raped by a cab driver. He was a good-looking, friendly young black man. We began talking about Aretha Franklin's records, among other things, and I suddenly realized that he was headed in the wrong direction. When I asked where he was going, he said that he had to pick up his wife from work at a certain time and if he carried me home first he would be late getting her.

Then he joked, "You know how you wives are if we are fifteen minutes late and you have to stand and wait."

We both laughed about that, because he was right. So I told him that it was all right and I wasn't in a hurry.

However, I noticed that he was heading toward Hilton Park. When I mentioned it, he didn't respond. I asked him again where his wife worked. Still, he didn't answer. Then I began to get suspicious, asking, "What are you trying to pull?"

He turned and said, "You know, you are a fine woman. I watched you walk toward this cab. I also saw you before you saw me. I circled the block hoping that you wouldn't get a cab before I could get back to pick you up."

I had been standing on the corner talking with some of the crowd from Bernie's. It wasn't unusual for us to stand and talk after the bars closed. He said, "You have a helluva walk, Miss. As soon as I saw you walk across the street, my dick got hard and I knew that I had to have some of that pussy."

My mind began racing, trying to think how I could get away from him. I knew I couldn't fight him off. It would be physically impossible. Although I hadn't seen him standing, the width of his shoulders and his height in the driver's seat made it clear that he was a strong man. He pulled into the park, stopped the cab in a remote, dark section and told me to undress.

I said, "O.K., if you don't mind getting the clap. Now, try explaining **that** to your wife."

He replied, "Who do you think you're kidding? I know you don't have the clap. Now take them damn clothes off so I can get a look at that fine body."

I tried very hard not to seem frightened. I wanted to sound as if I knew what was happening. I tried to talk like a prostitute. I began flirting with him and said, "O.K. handsome, I don't care if you don't. I wanted to fuck you as soon as I got in this cab and seen how good looking you is. You ain't even got to pay for this ass, Sugah, but when your ole lady starts whipping on your ass for giving her the clap remember I tried to warn you. I found out yesterday that I got the clap. Just one of the hazards of the trade, Baby. When you're in the business, you gotta roll with the punches. That's what we wuz talkin 'bout on the corner when you picked me up." I tried to talk real tough.

Then I began to unbutton my blouse, slowly, taking my time. I could tell he was thinking so I kept talking. "Whatcha want first?" I cooed in a sexy voice. "I gotta couple tricks I can show ya. You'll be sorry in the morning, but you'll have fun tu-nite. Whatta ya think I wuz doin in that section of town? I wuz hustling, Baby. I don't know none of them niggas down there. So what if they gets caught with the clap? Don't mean nothin ta me. They shouldn't been fishin widdout knowin the waters. I gots kids at home ta feed. My man is in jail. I needs de money, Sugah."

He didn't know whether to believe me or not. Obviously, he thought it was better to be safe than sorry. He looked at me real hard and said, "I don't know whether to take a chance or not."

He must have changed his mind because he backed the cab out of the park and was still puzzled over what I had said. He drove slowly up North Avenue, obviously thinking hard about what I had said. At a traffic light he turned to me and said, "I don't believe you. I can see how you carry yourself and besides, you're too clean looking to have the clap. You don't look like no whore and when we wuz talking when you first got in my cab, you didn't sound like no whore. I believe you been lying to me. I think I'll call your bluff."

When he said that, I jumped out of the cab and ran in the opposite direction. He made a U-turn in the middle of the street, but not before I had a chance to run up a one-way street. I was afraid to stop another cab. I had run into a little side street off North Avenue. I didn't know the name of the street so I couldn't have said where I was even if I did have someone to call to come get me, which I didn't.

I stood in the doorway of a row house. It was a neat little house with green and white awnings over the windows and doors with the initial "M" on them. I could tell that the occupants were homeowners rather than renters because of the way the house was maintained. The doors were of heavy, maple-colored wood.

The traditional Baltimore white marble steps were scrubbed so clean that one could have eaten from them. The windows were clean and the doorway smelled of fresh pine scent.

I stood there for what seemed to be hours, and watched the night turn into dawn, afraid to go back into the streets. The milkman came and left a bottle of milk and a loaf of fresh bread just inside the doorway. The paper boy came and left the newspaper. I was chilled in the crisp morning air, but I was still too scared to leave the protective doorway.

When the neighborhood began to come alive with activity, the door opened. By that time I was crying, wondering what to do. A little old lady with her white hair pinned neatly into a bun on top of her head, wearing a housecoat and slippers came out to get the milk, bread, and paper. When she saw me, she looked at me for a long time without saying a word. I was crying softly. Then she smiled and said, "Child, you're shivering. You must be cold. How long you been standing out here?"

"All night," I answered. I could no longer control the tears I had been trying so hard to control all night for fear that I would cry so loudly that someone might hear me and call the police.

The kind old lady asked, "Are you hurt? Are you all right?"

"Yes, ma'am. I just want to get home to my children."

I told her what had happened. She was so nice, she just listened without interrupting me. She offered me breakfast. I told her that I appreciated her kindness, but I just wanted to get home. By that time the buses had started running, so I caught a bus and went home.

Gayle was still there with the children as I knew she would be. She was such a good friend. She was more like a younger sister to me than a babysitter. She took care of the children as if they were her own. Maybe that was why God had sent her to me. He knew I needed someone to depend on while I was in the streets trying to cope with life.

When I arrived home, the kids were just sitting down to the breakfast that Gayle had prepared for them. As usual, no one had heard from Jerry. I hadn't seen him since he left home Friday morning for work, and now it was Sunday. So, what else was new?

Another World

When I went to Boston with Butchie to stay with my sister while Jerry was recuperating in North Carolina, I got an education about another way of life: prostitution.

I was fascinated by the pimps and whores, their lifestyles and the excitement of nightlife. Sandy operated an after-hours club in her home. After the nightclubs and bars closed, the nighttime "in-crowd" eventually ended up at Sandy's.

At the time, Sandy was living with Raymond, who was not especially handsome, but he knew all about nightlife and he knew how to "make a dollar." He tried to talk Sandy and me into becoming prostitutes and he would be our pimp. No one would prostitute without a pimp in those days. If you were an "independent whore," other pimps, johns, and even the police would hassle you, beat you, rob you, and make hustling very hard. Therefore, prostitutes needed pimps for protection. The pimps didn't allow their prostitutes to keep any of the money they earned, nor were they allowed to have a bank account.

A prostitute was rated by the amount of money she could make in one night. It was common to make no less than $250 a night on Thursdays and Fridays, and $500 on Saturdays and Sundays just walking the streets and picking up johns.

I watched the women walk the streets in their mini-skirts. A john would drive by, and after negotiating, the prostitute would get into his car. They would leave and after about twenty minutes or so, the john would return and the prostitute would get out of the car and resume walking her beat.

When I wouldn't prostitute myself, Raymond decided to hassle me. He decided to force me to pay half the rent, half the utility bills, and buy half the groceries. It didn't matter that I was only visiting. He wanted to force me into "the life" even though I had come to Boston to get a job.

I thought that when Jerry was better, if we moved away from Baltimore and started a new life together, our marriage might have a better chance for survival. Sandy had asked me to come to Boston and she said that I could live with her until I found a job. However, Raymond saw a way of making fast money, he thought.

Sandy and Raymond got into fights that reminded me of Mother and Frank. They really tried to hurt each other. They were jealous and always accused each other of having affairs with other people. One night while they were fighting, Sandy stabbed Raymond with an ice pick. When we realized how badly he was hurt, one of the guests drove him to the hospital. We followed in Sandy's car. When we arrived, Raymond was on a stretcher waiting to be seen. When he saw Sandy, he tried to hit her and the blood squirted out of his wound like water out of a faucet. Because he had been drinking, the blood flowed faster.

I was tired of the fights, of the crowd, and of my son staying with people I didn't know. He was such a good child. He was only three years old, yet he never cried, never gave me any trouble, always smiling. When he cut his foot stepping on a broken soda bottle, it took stitches to close the wound. I cried harder than he did. He was walking on the foot the following day, stitches and all.

One night Sandy and I were at a night club where I met Ronnie, Boston's number one pimp. He said, "Hello, my name is Ronnie. I am rich and you are beautiful. I'll keep you beautiful and you can keep me rich. Order what you want and put it on my tab."

I looked at him and said over my shoulder as I walked away, "I didn't need your help to become beautiful. I don't need your help to stay beautiful. If I make anyone rich, it will be me. I'm afraid you are out of your league."

Ronnie was a very handsome man, and he wasn't accustomed to women talking to him in that manner. However, my obvious lack of interest intrigued him. The more I ignored him, the more he pursued me. He and I became good friends after he decided that the only way to befriend me was to drop that pimp bullshit.

I told him that I was looking for a job and was to be interviewed at the Prudential Insurance Company the following Monday. I also told him that my ultimate goal was to finish college. We became friends because he respected me. I was different from the prostitutes he was accustomed to being with.

I would often ride with him to "check his traps," that is to make sure that his prostitutes were "working" (walking the streets). He even had prostitutes "working" in Atlantic City, long before the casinos were built. Once he said, "I have a lot of cows in my stable," meaning that he had lots of whores working for him. He owned a grocery store, a record store, and a dry cleaning company. He wore fabulous clothes and jewelry, and he drove a Cadillac - all with money from his prostitutes.

His friends didn't like Ronnie spending time with me, because I was a "square broad." I was hired as a clerk by the Prudential Insurance Company and I was excited about it. One day after work,

I was sitting in Ronnie's car talking with him. He liked to talk with me about school, my plans, my home life, and so on. It was hard for his friends to understand that we were just good friends.

One of his buddies walked up to the car and said, "Hello Ronnie. I see you have a new lady."

Then he said to me, "I bet you are a five-hundred-a-night whore, too, because you're a fine looking mama. You're new in town, ain't you?"

I said, very indignantly, "I am not a whore."

The friend said, "Are you a booster?" Meaning, did I steal and sell stolen goods?

"No, I am not a booster."

"Are you a Thursday woman?"

Thursday women were live-in maids for white families. Their days off were every Thursday and every other weekend. They gave pimps their money just as the prostitutes did, because it was a status symbol to be associated with a good- looking pimp, ride in a fancy car, and hang out at the best places with the "in- crowd."

I said, "No, I am not a Thursday woman."

"Then what are you? What do you do?"

It never occurred to him that I might work for a living. I said with obvious pride, "I work for Prudential."

I was really proud of getting the job so soon after arriving in Boston. However, the friend did not see it that way, He looked at me, frowned, and said, "You mean you are a nine-to-five woman? You mean you are a "square" broad?

"Ronnie," he said, "you mean you're actually spending time with a woman who works for a living? Are you recruiting her?"

Before Ronnie had a chance to respond, I said, "No, he is not recruiting me."

The friend told Ronnie he was messing up his image being seen with me, and he walked away. After that, whenever I saw that friend, he avoided me. He was seriously upset, because I was a legitimate working woman. Ronnie took a lot of kidding from his friends about me. I wanted to work and go to college. Again, I didn't fit in.

Sandy left Raymond and she and I got an apartment, but she and Raymond went back together and I was left living alone. I had decided to work, save some money, and go get my girls. When Jerry was back to good health, we would already have an apartment. We would just have our furniture shipped to Boston, I thought.

Then I received a letter telling me that Jerry was back in the hospital and a neighbor was taking care of my children. I took a leave of absence from Prudential intending to return once I had gotten my girls. But as you have read, that was not to be.

Frank

In 1958, while I was a student at Morgan State, Mother, Al, Sandy, and Frank moved to Washington D.C. Frank got a job as a security guard at a large shopping mall. He often got "hot" clothes from junkies. He didn't steal them, he just looked the other way while employees of various mall stores stole them. They would give some of the clothes to Frank as payment. Most of the stores carried only men's and boy's clothes. However, the sweaters and coats could be worn by both sexes.

Frank came to Baltimore one weekend to visit me and my family and bought some clothes for my children. When Mother found out about it, she said to Frank, "From now on make Barbran pay for the things you give her, but don't charge Sandy for anything, because Barbran got a husband and Sandy don't." It didn't matter that Jerry and I were struggling financially. It didn't matter that we needed all the help we could get. The only thing that seemed to matter was that Frank should not do me any favors.

Sandy was always the one at home and well taken care of. I was the one left to fend for myself. When I left home for college, Sandy was living at Maelizzie's house with Mother and Al. Frank was in the brig for forgery. When he was released, they all moved to Washington together. I had wanted to go home for the Christmas holidays just like everyone else on Morgan's campus. However, once I left Georgia to go to college I never went home again. I didn't have money for train fare and Mother didn't send me any. In fact, after Mother, Sandy and Al went to live with Maelizzie and Bob, I never received any assistance from my family. I was totally on my own.

When Mother, Al, Sandy, and Frank moved to DC, Mother would tell me about how Frank was still beating her, but she would never leave him. I would try to convince her to come and live with me, but every time we talked about it she turned on me. She acted as if I were trying to break up her marriage.

She would say, "Don't be trying to get me to leave my husband. You are still with yours."

I would say, "Yes, but mine doesn't beat me. Mother, one day one of you will kill the other."

She would tell me to mind my business and leave hers alone. Yet, she told me how he had beaten her so badly one time that he had broken two of her ribs. She couldn't walk up stairs to the bedroom or the bathroom. She lay on the sofa for two days, begging Frank to take her to the hospital, but he refused. Finally, on the third day, when one of Al's girlfriends came to visit him, she saw that Mother was hurt and took her to the hospital.

A few months later Frank began coughing up phlegm mixed with blood. Mother tried to get him to go to the hospital, but he refused. His throat hurt him so badly one day that he went to the doctor for medicine, which was unusual for him. The doctor tried to get him to go on a diet, but Frank said no; he wanted to stay a "big man."

Frank's cough had become progressively worse. Mother begged him to go to the hospital but Frank was afraid of hospitals and doctors and he refused to go. Instead, he kept coughing and spitting into a brown paper bag. His throat was so sore he had difficulty swallowing even his own saliva. Consequently, he began to lose a lot of weight rapidly.

Mother went onto the front porch where Frank was sitting one day and found him unconscious. Because he was so big, he sometimes had difficulty breathing while lying down. Therefore, he often slept sitting in a chair either in the living room or on the front porch. He had become a common figure to the neighbors by sitting on the porch sleeping and snoring so loudly that he could be heard almost half a block away.

Mother, missing his snores, realized that something was wrong. She found him with his eyes closed, and his head dropped backward resting on the back of the metal porch chair. She tried to awaken him but couldn't. That's when she realized that something was wrong. She immediately called an ambulance and they carried him to the hospital. We later learned that he was suffering from throat cancer and Mother had found him just in time to save his life.

Frank gave the doctors and nurses in the hospital a fit, to say the least. He was their most disagreeable patient. He constantly cursed the nurses and doctors and sometimes he had to be restrained just so they could treat him. In addition, he constantly used profanity in the presence of hospital visitors.

Jerry, Butch, Jeanene, Jeanese, my granddaughter, and I went to DC so that the family could visit Frank. (Jericka was an FBI agent based in Tennessee and couldn't leave). Mother tried to convince me to go with the rest of the family. I refused. I kept asking myself what I would say to him once I was there. I disliked the man so intensely for what he had done to my mother and to me that I couldn't pretend that I was truly concerned about his health.

My family went to the hospital without me. Frank asked why I had not come and they told him I stayed home to take care of the baby, my granddaughter, so that the rest of the family could visit him.

Frank stayed in the hospital for approximately three weeks. When he was released, he was instructed to continue his treatments by keeping his weekly appointments, but he never went once. Instead, he went back to work, still coughing. He didn't tell his co-workers that he was sick and had been confined to the hospital. Instead, he said that he had been out of town on vacation with his family.

I also learned that when Sandy came to Washington to visit him, he started crying and asking why I disliked him and why I didn't visit him while he was in the hospital. "I ain't never did nothing to Barbran," he sobbed, "I don't see why she treats me like that."

I didn't feel guilty about Frank crying. He was always good with tears. I can remember how he would beat Mother and then start crying when we came to her defense, crying about how he was mistreated. Mother could be standing there with her eye swollen shut, her lip swollen, and blood all over her where he had used her as a punching bag, while he stood crying, trying to convince Sandy and me how badly he was mistreated. Something was wrong with that picture. He could cry real tears easier than the average woman. "Crocodile tears," Mother called them. Oh, he was good, real good.

Frank continued to refuse to go to the hospital for treatment. Mother said she was putting him in the hands of the Lord. "All I can do is pray for him. I know that prayer works," she said. "It worked for me. When the doctors told me that I had cancer and only had a year to live, I promised God that if He would heal my body and make me well again, I would spend the rest of my life working for Him."

In fact, it did work for her. She lost that bloatedness. Her hair grew back prettier and a better grade than it had been before the treatments. Instead of needing treatment every week, she was required to take them only once every other month, until gradually she didn't have to take them at all.

Frank was not a religious man, although, when we were growing up, he and Mother went to church every other Sunday and he would make us go every Sunday. If we didn't go to Sunday school, we were not allowed to leave the backyard all day Sunday. Now that he and Mother were older and going through the "empty nest syndrome," he drove her to church and back, but he never went inside. He even refused to attend his granddaughter's wedding, which was held in the same church, although his cousin was the pastor and his other relatives had helped to build the church.

Mother always said that he was Satan and Satan is afraid to enter God's House. Now here he was, crying again trying to get sympathy, telling everyone how badly I had mistreated him by not going to visit him while he was in the hospital.

Less than two months after Frank was released from the hospital, Mother called me in Baltimore and said, "Barbran, he's gone. Frank is gone." By then she had long since stopped referring to him as my father, because she knew how much I disliked it.

Frank had been dressing for work. He had put on his pants and was sitting on the side of the bed, putting on his shoes and socks and he just lay back, closed his eyes, and died. He had one shoe on and a sock in his hand, with his shirt on the bed beside him when Mother found him.

The poor preacher tried to find something good to say about him during the funeral service. He talked about how Frank would "speak his mind."

I cried real hard at the funeral. I wasn't crying because Frank was dead, I cried for what could have been. I cried for all the mental and physical pain Frank had caused my mother for almost fifty years. I cried because she was not strong enough to leave him. I cried for all the hate that had grown and festered inside me. I cried because the grandchildren and the great-grandchildren had been deprived of the love of their grandfather and great-grandfather. I cried because the wisdom that is possessed by the elderly had been denied his family. I cried because he could have been a very loving and caring father. I cried because that was the only way I could release the hurt.

Frank owned a red 1980 Cadillac. He loved that big car. After the church service, on the way to the cemetery, Mother had the funeral procession drive past their house. She said that she wanted Frank to "see" the car he loved one last time.

Although Frank had gotten into trouble while he was in the army, he was still given a military funeral with the guns fired in salute and Taps blown by the bugler. Mother was presented with the American flag that had been draped over his casket.

Tribute to a Great Lady

After Frank died, Mother's health deteriorated. Sandy called Mother every day to check on her. Each day after Sandy called mother, she would call me at the office to discuss mother's health. One day she called Mother and kept getting a busy signal. After about two hours of this, Sandy called my brother's former wife, Cathy. Although Cathy was divorced from my brother, she was such a wonderful person that we still thought of her as our sister-in-law. Sandy asked if she had talked with Mother that day. Cathy said she had not spoken with Mother but she would ask one of the neighbors to go knock on Mother's door.

The neighbor called Cathy back to say that she had knocked on the door, but no one answered it. The phone was still giving a busy signal and this prompted Cathy to call the police. The police met her at Mother's house. When they arrived, they found the doors locked from the inside. They broke the lock on the back door and went inside.

They found Mother in the upstairs bedroom. She was disoriented, dehydrated, and incoherent. The telephone had fallen to the floor. Mother had suffered a stroke and had tried to call for help, but couldn't hold the phone. She was immediately rushed to the hospital where she stayed for about a month.

Mother had cancer for a year before I found out about it. My sister-in-law had been taking her back and forth to the hospital for chemotherapy treatments. Al had found Mother lying on the sofa, hardly able to breathe. He carried her to the hospital and she was diagnosed as having cancer.

She had made my sister-in-law promise not to tell Sandy or me. At first I was angry with my sister-in-law for keeping that kind of information from me; after all, she was my mother. Then I realized that my sister-in-law was in a tough position because she was living in Mother's house.

The doctors said that Cathy found Mother just in time. She was so severely dehydrated that another half-hour might have been too late. After that, she was partially paralyzed in her right arm, dragged her left leg, and had to have oxygen constantly. A woman was to come each day to stay with her, but the lady wasn't dependable. I tried to get Mother to live with me, but she was too independent. She wanted to live alone. She asked me and her pastor to check on senior citizens homes for her. However, the doctor said she couldn't take care of herself.

Mother fought us every way she could so that she could live by herself. She talked about how traumatic it would be to leave all of her belongings behind and move in with someone else, even if that some-one else happened to be her daughter. I could understand Mother's feelings, but she couldn't take care of herself and we couldn't afford to pay for full-time care.

We asked Mother if she had given up the will to live because of Frank's death? She said, yes, because she wanted to be with him. She thought that she had heard him call her name one night after he died.

For a while, Mother did all right. Then after a year, almost on the anniversary of Frank's death, she suffered a heart attack. With the cancer spreading through her body, the stroke, the partial paralysis, and then the heart attack, the doctors insisted that she could not live alone. Despite the trauma of leaving the house she had shared with Frank, she realized that her health had taken a turn for the worse.

After Sandy and I discussed the situation with the doctor, we decided that Mother would have to live with one of us. I wanted Mother to live with me and Sandy wanted Mother to live with her. Therefore, we decided to let Mother decide. If she lived with me, her bedroom would have been on the second floor with the bathroom on the first floor. She didn't think she would be able to walk up and down the stairs, so she chose to live with Sandy.

I didn't object, knowing that Sandy was at home more than me. Also, Sandy's children were still at home and they would be good company for Mother. It didn't matter where she stayed, as long as I could talk to her, see her when I wanted to, and as long as she was all right.

This was unlike my household, where everyone was involved in various activities at school, work, or church, and they were about to move into apartments of their own. Also, the older Sandy got, the more she became like Frank in her physical features, including her voice, mannerisms, and size. Mother could see Frank in Sandy and actually started calling Sandy by the nickname she had called Frank for almost fifty years. Sandy was Frank's real daughter.

Mother knew how much I disliked Frank because of the way he had treated her all those years. She couldn't keep Frank's memory alive living with me because I wouldn't talk with her about him. I couldn't reminisce about the "good times" and pretend to miss him as she and Sandy could and would do. After all the hurt, after all the pain, after all the betrayals, after all the abuse, after all the insults, Mother still loved him.

Later, Mother seemed to change towards me. Maybe it was my imagination, I hope so. Sometimes I noticed Mother and Sandy discussing things secretly and when I entered the room they would stop talking. I found out that Mother had been sending Sandy money to pay Sandy's rent, but both of them had kept that from me. I only found out about it because when Sandy's mail was late, I overheard them discussing it together in the hospital.

Maybe it was my imagination again, but when she and Sandy were leaving for Boston I could have sworn that Mother turned her head from me when I tried to kiss her good-bye. Al and Sandy were surrounding Mother as she was talking and laughing with them and ignoring me. She became agitated and responded in a snappy voice every time I said something to her. I don't know why she changed towards me. Sometimes I felt that because she missed Frank so deeply and because Al and Sandy were Frank's natural children, she felt closer to them, and in that way, closer to Frank.

Sandy and Al always thought of me as the strongest of the three of us, the one who could handle the problems. When Mother wouldn't take her medicine, they called me. Whenever anything went wrong, they called me. But the truth was, I was the most sensitive. I pretended to be strong, because I knew they needed that show of strength. But when I was alone I cried like a baby. Sometimes, I walked the streets crying and talking to myself and to God. The passers-by must have thought I was crazy.

The doctors had given Mother less than a year to live. We had been trying to get her to stop drinking for years, to no avail. She would stop for a few days and then return to the alcohol. I even promised to drive to Washington once a week to go with her to Alcoholics Anonymous meetings. We attended one meeting together and she attended one meeting alone, then she didn't go again. She told me later that she stopped attending because Frank wouldn't go with her.

When Mother was in the hospital, the doctor called Sandy in Boston to tell her that Mother was in such bad shape that she wouldn't leave the hospital alive without a miracle. He said he wanted to prepare us for the worst. Mother had said, "I walked in and I will walk out with the help of God." The preacher from Mother's church came and prayed over her.

The Bishop, his wife, and Elders from Sandy's church who were in Baltimore attending a conference came to the hospital to visit Mother. We held hands around her bed and prayed for her. They said, "Satan, you don't have any business here. This woman belongs to God. You get out of this room and leave God's child alone." Mother walked out of the hospital!

Mother dressed very well. She was a good-looking woman and she kept a clean house. She was mugged and robbed once in Washington. Someone hit her in her head and snatched her purse, when she was drunk, but it never dampened her spirit.

Once when Mother hadn't heard from me in two weeks, she read in the paper that a black female had been floating in a river in Baltimore. She caught a cab, went to the Greyhound bus station, bought a round-trip ticket to Baltimore, and came to see if I was all right. She often did that. She would go to the store for a loaf of bread and when she didn't return in a reasonable time, Frank would call me in Baltimore and ask, "Is your mother there?" She always would be there. She would just decide that she wanted to see me, keep right on going, get a train or a bus and come to Baltimore to see me - no luggage, no change of clothes, nothing but love. She would always tell me when she finally arrived at my house, "I just wanted to see your face and just touch you."

Sometimes it was the wee hours of the night and sometimes it was during the day. The time did not matter. When she wanted to see her daughter, she came just like she was. That was my mother.

When people ask me who inspires me, who do I admire most,

or who is really my hero, I never have to stop and think about my answer. Immediately I respond by saying, "My mother." She was the strongest woman I ever knew. She might not have been physically strong, but she certainly was emotionally the strongest person I had ever met. Who else could have suffered the pain and humiliation that she did from one man, and remain?

Who else, deprived by her husband of the material wealth that was rightfully hers would rarely complain and refuse to leave him? After going through all that mental torture, she still found time and reasons to praise her God. She still found time to help others. She still found time to care. She still found time to teach us the meaning of love and forgiveness, the value of an education, and moral and ethical values. She was a beautiful woman.

She never stole, she never lied, and she never made a promise she didn't keep. If she felt that she could not keep a promise, she refused to make one. She often said, "If a person will lie, he or she will steal, and I don't want nothing I don't work for."

She and Frank often got into arguments about the clothes Frank would get from the junkies. Mother considered it wrong, although Frank wasn't doing the stealing himself.

She was beautiful physically, spiritually, emotionally, and ethically. Alcohol, although it consumed most of her life, could not completely claim her. Each time she and I talked, I discovered a different quality in her. She was like a child. I enjoyed simple things with her like visiting an amusement park or discovering simple enjoyments often taken for granted, such as the expression on a clown's face, or rides on a ferris wheel. I enjoyed the world so much through her eyes. God looked deep into her soul and saw what we could not see, snatched her from Satan, and said, "Get thee behind me Satan. This woman belongs to me."

For so many years I was angry with her because I felt she cheated me out of a "normal" childhood. I would imagine having loving parents as did some of my friends. How I envied them for having a "real family." How wrong I was. I wish I had known how to handle alcoholism at that time. Maybe I could have helped her to endure the pain inflicted on her by society, which at that time, neither understood nor was tolerant of alcoholism or the alcoholic.

Sandy called me at 3 a.m. to tell me that Mother had gotten worse during the night and she had taken her to the hospital. After the hospital had admitted Mother, Sandy knelt beside her bed to pray with her. Mother told Sandy to leave the room because "Doctor Jesus" was in the room and she wanted to be alone with Him. She died that night, smiling.

Later the same night, the hospital called Sandy and said that when the doctor went into Mother's room they noticed that she had begun to breathe again! Sandy rushed back to the hospital. The doctors had Mother connected to life-support machines. They called me and asked me to give the authorization to disconnect the machines. I refused. How could I tell them to let my mother die? But God in His Mercy intervened and made the decision for us. Mother went peacefully.

The American Dream

To have overcome sexual molestation by my stepfather; being an illegitimate child, being physically abused by an alcoholic mother and my stepfather; winning a personal battle with drugs; being on welfare; growing up in the streets; living in the projects; surviving a marriage with a husband who was constantly unfaithful and who was a heavy gambler; having four babies born within the same year, a set of triplets and a single birth all in the same year; having two strikes against me, being Black and a female; to go from being a miserably unhappy creature to a Christian; and to become a successful business owner is the American dream.

For a long time I thought that I was ten years behind the time. I kept thinking that where I am today professionally, educationally, and financially, I should have been ten years ago. I often felt that ten years of my life had been wasted because I was a product of the streets.

Now, I realize that I am exactly where I should be at this time in my life. I needed time to build a business, which required long hours and offered little pay. I needed time to go to PTA meetings when my children were in school. I needed to be there to attend little league games and watch my son play ball. I needed to take my daughters to majorette practice. I needed to come home and cook dinner for my family. I could not have done all that and built a business too. My mind was not ready for the psychological discipline that building a business required. I was young, and I wanted to be in the streets, having a good time with my friends.

We have all heard the American dream story; the story of someone's big success in business, the overnight success. The person may have made $75,000 within the first month of business, may have had sales of over one million dollars the first two years, and so forth. It wasn't like that for me.

I decided to start a training and development firm specializing in creating training programs for managers, supervisors, and first level employees. Our programs also included Employee Assistance training. At the end of my first six months in business I still could not afford the $3.75 needed to park my car on the lot behind my office building. I carried two sets of car keys with me. One set I left with the parking attendant so that he could move my car if it was blocking another car. If I didn't get my car before the parking lot closed, the attendant locked my car keys in the office and I couldn't get them until the following day.

However, I often purposely waited until the lot closed, then I would use my extra keys to drive home because I didn't have the $3.75. I would borrow it from Jerry and pay the attendant the next day. It became so common that the attendant expected me to pay him later.

At the end of the first year I was faced with replacing carpet and supplies that an office-mate, whom I had considered a friend, took from me. I guess you could compare me with a turtle, slow and deliberate. So many times I wanted to give up and get a job working for someone else, but my pride wouldn't allow me to admit failure. And besides, once a person gets a taste of working without so much "red tape," and "calling the shots" on his or her own time, it's hard to go back to working for someone else.

Jerry kept saying, "A lot of people try it and can't make a go of it. It's not embarrassing to give up the idea of being a business owner and go to work for someone else."

But he was wrong. It would have been embarrassing to me. I kept praying and kept having faith that my prayers would be answered. God said all you need is faith the size of a mustard seed and you can move mountains.

I started working in an entry level grade 0 position at the Municipal Court in Baltimore Maryland in 1967. I responded to an job advertisement and was notified to report for an interview. I got the job making only $60 per week and brought home $90 every two weeks. The money didn't matter that much. What mattered most was that I had a job. Although racism and discrimination were rampant within the Baltimore court system in the 1960s, eventually I was able to move up to the level of Deputy Administrator of the Circuit Court.

Being Deputy Administrator of the Circuit Court was considered a "good" job in those days, especially for a black woman. I received a regular paycheck every two weeks, plus benefits. If I was out sick, I still received a paycheck. If I wanted time off, I was entitled to a month's vacation with pay, plus personal leave. In other words, I was in a very comfortable position, with salary and benefits totaling approximately $75,000 annually; yet, I was unhappy working there.

I had always dreamed of owning my own business "someday." My daughter Jericka and I had talked of "someday" opening a clinic and vocational rehabilitation center for ex-offenders and for individuals with histories of being welfare recipients, concentrating on women heads-of-households with dependent children.

I talked of "someday" completing my doctorate. I spoke of "someday," always somewhere in the future. I didn't feel the need to plan for "someday" today. My job with the court system was like a security blanket for me. I always had a safe, secure feeling with a steady salary and benefits. When you work for someone else your needs are automatically met. When you work for yourself, everything begins and ends with you.

People often ask me if it was difficult for a person who was accustomed to working for someone else to start a business? My answer is, "Yes, very difficult." I didn't know the meaning of the word "entrepreneur."

Your body will let you know when it is time to change your environment. When that happens, listen to the warning messages. I am glad I listened to mine. I was a reasonably healthy person, yet I began to have headaches after I had been Deputy Administrator of the Circuit Court for about four years.

The headaches became so severe that I went to my doctor, and he couldn't determine what was causing them. He referred me to a local hospital, where tests were run for two days trying to determine the cause of my headaches. I also developed a rash on my face for which I was referred to a dermatologist. Finally, my doctor decided that I should see a neurologist.

Discussing the rash one day, my doctor listed my week's activities and compiled a list of the foods I had eaten that week. As the doctor and I were discussing the lists, we noticed an emerging pattern. I only had the headaches Mondays through Fridays, every week. I never had them on weekends, never on holidays, and never on my days off from work. Not only that, the rash cleared up on the weekends and returned on Mondays, then lasted all week. My doctor informed me that I was experiencing the effects of stress.

"Stress?" I said in disbelief. "I don't have stress. Nothing stresses me. I am too vocal to experience stress. If you don't believe me, just check my personnel file for the past years."

He said, "Something is stressing you and it's apparently associated with your employment, because your symptoms only appear during work hours."

After much discussion, I was convinced that he was correct. We concluded that the job that I had once loved and had now come to hate was causing me stress. When I was first appointed to the position of Deputy Administrator of the Supreme Bench, I loved the challenge of the position.

It wasn't long, however, before I realized that I was a mere figurehead. I was someone to whom the courts could point saying that they had a minority person in a responsible position. When I realized that the job was stressing me, I knew that I had to make a decision. It took me three months to make that decision.

People often ask me why I didn't stay and fight the system because right was on my side. When that question comes up, I tell them that I had been fighting the system and its prejudice for eighteen years. I had watched the system methodically discriminate against not only black employees, but other minorities as well.

I can remember when I was disciplined by a white supervisor at the District Court because she told me to, "Tell the Jew lady to leave."

When I asked why, the supervisor said, "Because she doesn't fit in."

When I refused, I was denied a promotion. When I filed a grievance and was later given the promotion, the same supervisor said, "Aren't you going to thank me?"

I said, "For what? You only gave me what I earned."

What she didn't know was that I knew that two of us were up for promotions, a white female and I, and there were two openings of equal rank. However, the white employee was to be promoted into one position and the other was to be downgraded before I was promoted into it.

I learned that when the supervisor said the Jewish woman didn't fit in, she was looking for a reason to fire her due to the number of Jewish holidays. Therefore, the supervisor was attempting to get me to do her dirty work. I heard those same words at the Circuit Court about a black woman, "She doesn't fit in."

I was tired of fighting. I was working in the court system when black employees were encouraged to use toilets separate from the white employees. I was working there when women were fighting for the right to wear slacks and pants suits to work, even though we sometimes were required to stoop, bend, and or climb ladders when filing and getting supplies. I was fighting for the right of black employees to wear the natural hair style, although the white employees were allowed to wear their hair natural, just wash it, brush it, and go. Yet white supervisors were telling me to do something to my hair.

The [white] system didn't seem to know or care that the hair texture of some black people is different than that of white people. What is natural to us is not necessarily natural to them. As Blacks, we were encouraged to "straighten our nappy hair." I was fighting the system when white employees were promoted and black employees were overlooked, although they worked side-by-side with the white employees and did the same work. I was just tired of fighting.

I realized that I could have filed a complaint with the Equal Employment Opportunity Commission or with the Human Relations Commission. But what would that have accomplished except to keep a job that I had grown to hate? The Administrative Judge could have relocated my office and reassigned my duties to do whatever he wanted, as long as I was performing his definition of "administrative functions."

Whenever anyone inquired about the court's Affirmative Action Policy, minority participation, and black representation in management positions, I was held up to the public and the media to send the message, *See, we have met our quota. We have a black woman in the number-two position with the court.* I was tired of trying to please judges who were obviously more interested in politics than in justice. No, it was time for me to leave.

On the day I resigned, I said to my supervisor, "The only thing that you or any of these judges can take from me is this job, and I was working when I got this job. You cannot take away my experience. I have been fighting racism all of my life. The battle does not change, the fight does not change, the game does not change. The only things that change are the opponents, the rules, and the players. Today becomes the tomorrow that I worried about yesterday. I can take the skills, education, and training that I acquired over the years and work for myself."

Afterwards, I felt a calmness that I hadn't felt since I accepted the position with the court. I felt an excitement, an adventurous kind of excitement, as if I were a little apprehensive as we usually are when facing changes, but I wasn't afraid. I knew that God was on my side. I had walked those streets surrounding the court house many times, crying and talking to God.

Evidently God meant for Jerry and me to be together because despite our own destructive behavior and other efforts to break us up, we have been together for over thirty years. Jerry is now my biggest supporter no matter what I endeavor. He encourages me to become whatever I want to become. I look back on those rough years and wonder how we ever made it, and I know that it was only with the help of God.

We could not have become the people we are today without the struggle and sacrifice. We both understand each other's needs and we are sensitive to each other's hurts and disappointments. I am sorry we had to grow through all the pain, but I thank God we survived. When we go to church as a family and I look at my handsome husband sitting beside me, I smile to myself and I silently thank God for making us the people we are today.

I was so proud of my children then and I am still proud of them now. I wish I could turn back the hands of time and have more time to enjoy their childhood years. I spent so much time being angry and stressed that I really didn't enjoy my family as much as I could have.

Each of my children has a different personality and each one brings me joy. Jeanese is funny and makes me laugh all the time. She is a very caring and sensitive person. If I had listened to one of her high school counselors, Jeanese would never have graduated from college. The counselor asked me to attend a meeting with her at school. She told me, "We both know that Jeanese is not college material. Instead of encouraging her to go to college, let's see if we can find a good trade school for her so that she can get a job and find a husband."

I was absolutely furious with her for trying to define my daughter's limitation. I gave her a piece of my mind and I never had to worry about that counselor again. Jeanese could be whatever she wanted to be, it just meant working a little harder for it. She is now working on her second degree, she teaches school, and she signs in church for those in the congregation who are hearing impaired.

Jeanene is the one who likes to party and have a good time. She is the one who is friendly and likes to meet people. But my greatest blessing is that all my children belong to a church. In addition, Jeanene is the one who has given me beautiful grandchildren.

Butchie, my only son, is my pride and joy. He is studying accounting and he is the bookkeeper for my company. He has a great speaking voice and has won many trophies for his oratorical skills.

Jericka is a FBI agent. She has always made me proud. She went to college on a scholarship, and she broke one of the records for the hurdles at the FBI Academy. She graduated with honors from school and college, and she is just like her mother.

All of my children's names begin with a "J." That's because I love my husband.

Sister, You are not Alone

Reading the newspaper one day, I thought I was reading about myself and I said, "Sister, you are not alone! I have been there." When I read in the first paragraph that you hit your children, are mean to them, have no patience with them, curse them, call them names, and then go somewhere by yourself and cry because you are really sorry, I can identify with what you are feeling. I feel your anguish, because I have been there - even when they were just playing, just being children and would not go to bed without horsing around, "Ma, so-and-so hit me. Ma, make so-and-so stop. I did not. You did too," and so on.

You yell at them and then you begin to curse at them and call them names. You want to stop while you are doing it but you can't. You just keep yelling and cussing at them. Finally, when you have vented your rage, you wonder why you said those things. They didn't do anything to deserve that type of treatment, especially from their mother. Then you begin noticing that your children shy away from you when you try to touch them. They are unresponsive when you try to hug them. They seem to be afraid of you. They go out of their way to try to please you so that you won't get angry with them.

Your husband doesn't discipline the children when he is home, if he is home. If you have a husband who spends time at home with you and the children, you are lucky. If you are a single parent, you may still be lucky; at least you are spared the hurt from your spouse. You may not have the financial resources you want or need, but money isn't everything. Peace of mind is sometimes more important. I would have traded bread and water and life in a homeless shelter to living the life of hell that I did, suffering the beatings from my stepfather.

My children thought I was a "bad mama" because I was the disciplinarian. They thought that I was the meanest person in the world compared to their father, who didn't have the tasks of washing dirty diapers, smelly bed-sheets, and baby bottles, of sick babies vomiting sour milk all over their clothes and your clothes too, of dinners to prepare, the house to clean, dirty clothes to wash, children's hair to comb, ironing, no adult to talk to other than your neighbor, but who has time for social visits?

Maybe you work outside your home like I did. If that is the case, you have to perform all those chores after working eight hours. Yet, there is never money for little things like stockings, lipstick, a bra that really has clasps to fasten it instead of safety pins, and underpanties without holes. Sound familiar?

I've been there, thirty-two years ago, **and still, I cry.** I cry because the little things that once annoyed me when my own children were small and mischievous, now make me smile when I see them in my grandchildren. I cry because when I look at the closeness of my girlfriends and their adult children and grandchildren and I reflect on mine, I miss the closeness. I cry because I wasted so many precious years that I spent cussing and hitting my children when I should have been holding them, hugging them, kissing them, and just being glad that God gave me normal, healthy, intelligent, beautiful children.

I cry because I can see the fault in others that I could not see in myself and the children don't forget. They forgive, but rarely do they forget.

I cry because childhood is as quick as the pop of a camera's flashbulb and those precious moments only come around once in a lifetime and, once they are gone, they can never be regained and recaptured.

I cry because I realize now that I was treating my children as my mother had treated me. And she treated me as her father had treated her, and her father treated her as his father had treated him. I remember how I felt, the pain of feeling unwanted when I was subjected to the same type of treatment when I was a child. I often wondered what I had done to make my mother dislike me so much.

I never realized that it was the disease of alcoholism that was making her behave that way. Because that was the only way I knew how to respond to children, I brought those same abusing ways into the lives of my own children, and, God knows, "I love my kids."

I cry because when I stop and reflect on how I felt when I hugged my mother when I was a child, after she had either abused me verbally or physically and I knew that she was really sorry for what she had said or done, I could still feel the same hesitance in my own children's embrace when they hugged me.

I cry because after all is said and done, we only get one mother and the gift of motherhood is indeed a blessing. We can marry often and have many husbands and many wives and a number of children but we only get one mother and one father.

I cry because we only get one chance at being a parent to small children. By the time we learn how to be "good" parents, our children are grown and the impression we make on them when they are small will last into their adult years.

Understanding the pain, I say to you, Sisters, who are hurting to get help or seek counseling. If the place where you work has an Employee Assistance Program (EAP) contact the EAP counselor. If you do not have access to an EAP, call your local Social Services Department. Call somebody! Your children will thank you and you will eventually thank yourself.

You cannot do it alone because you are too close to the problem. When you feel the urge to curse your children and call them names, walk away. You will only hurt yourself and your children. I know you love them. I also know that once you get started it is very difficult to stop. Believe me, psychological scars last longer than physical scars. The pain of physical wounds will go away, but one will long remember the words that cut deeper than any blade, especially when those words come from the mouth of one's mother.

Hug your children. Childhood is so very brief. One day they are babies, the next day they are graduating from high school. You cannot recapture those precious years. I have wished so many times that I could live my life over again with the wisdom I have acquired with age. I would be there for my children, the mother they so desperately needed.

Take time and really look at the hurt and terror in the eyes of your children if you are abusing them. It's real. Put yourself in their place. Think about how you would feel if it were the other way around. Practice empathic understanding with your children. Walk in their shoes. The world looks so large and complicated through the eyes of small children.

Please, for the sake of your children, don't add to that confusion, that complication, and that fear. A mother should represent warmth, love, understanding, caring, and compassion. Be there for them. Remember, one day we too will grow old and will need to depend on the same people who now depend on us. Let them remember the love with which you cared for them. Let that same love guide them to want to care for you when your journey through life is nearing its end.

I cry because I cannot erase the pain I have caused my children. I cry because they cannot forget and neither can I. Yet, I cannot wallow in guilt and self-inflicted punishment. I have four children and they all have the same father and all had the same opportunities. They have to atone for their feelings. I must get on with my life. I cannot keep feeling guilty about that which guilt will not change.

I cry because all of the wisdom I needed in my youth, came only with maturity. I cry because the moments of despair I brought to my children cannot be erased. I cry because crying cannot erase the past and the present is filled with tears of the past. I cry because crying doesn't help...**and still, I cry.**

Epilogue

I don't know what tomorrow will bring. Nevertheless, I say to anyone reading this, follow your dream. Make a way out of no way. It's like how you eat an elephant, one bite at a time. Go after your dreams the same way, one step at a time. Don't ever give up. Don't let anyone define your limitations, and never affirm self-limitations. We are all unique. In all the history of the world there was never anyone else exactly like you, and in all the infinity to come, there will never be another you or another me. God made us all one-of-a-kind, and what you believe yourself to be, you are.

Initially I was embarrassed about having used drugs, being abused, being on welfare, promiscuity, and disloyalty, but those things made me stronger. Who can lead better than one who has been there? First-hand knowledge and experience rather than theories and concepts from books are much more effective in helping others who are traveling the same road I have already traveled. Street sense combined with education make a difficult team to beat.

The Bible tells us that we please God when we help each other. It teaches us that none of us are free until we all are free and that we are not living according to the Word of God until we are helping His people. I really believe those things, and now I can smile and say to myself as I look whence I came and how I came, "Lord, I don't know how I got over, but thank you for seeing me through, 'cause you brought me from a mighty long way, and I don't feel no ways tired."

Whatever your mind can conceive and believe, it can achieve. We have to dream great dreams and work to make them come true, but do it now. We only go around once in life, and this "ain't no practice run." This is the real thing - Now!

I have paid my dues. After all the hard knocks, after all the prejudice, after all the rejections, after all the pain, after all the acts of discrimination, I am still striving and making it. God is blessing me in my business; my children are successful and educated; my marriage has grown into what I wished it had been thirty years ago, but thank God I lived to see it mature and develop. God has blessed me with a loving husband of thirty-two years who has become my best friend.

Mother is not here to see my success; however, I am confident in the belief that she is still watching over me, smiling and saying, "Well done, daughter. Mother is proud of you." Each time I kneel to pray, I ask God to say "Hello" to Mother for me because I know she is flying around God's Throne, singing. She loved to sing, although she couldn't carry a tune in a bucket, but I know God is letting her sing...**and still, I cry.**

I cry because after over three hundred years, the black race is still not free. I cry because parents are killing children, children are killing parents, children are killing each other, and children are killing themselves.

I cry because some of us have many homes and some of us don't have a bed on which to sleep. I cry because some of us are obese and some of us are dying of hunger. I cry because some of us have many jobs, some of us don't want jobs, and some of us cannot find jobs.

I cry because racism and prejudice are still rampant in a nation that boasts of being the leader of the world. I cry because the black race is still judged by skin color rather than by capabilities. I cry because women are not yet equal to men, yet we are expected to "suffer peacefully." I cry because after all my struggles, after all my pain, I am still viewed as a black woman rather than as a competent business owner. I cry because I have to fight so hard to get things that come so easily to my white brothers and sisters and, to an extent, easier to my black brothers than to me and my black sisters.

I cry because I am expected to be grateful for crumbs when I earned the entire loaf. Even though one can forgive the battles as well as the wrongdoings, I cry because of the psychological scars that are left that no one can see, but those of us who are hurt, feel.

There are other times when I cry tears of happiness because God has given me the patience, tolerance, and the faith to endure troubles and obstacles that are placed in my path. I cry because God has taken away the guilt I felt because I could not undo the past. I cry tears of thanksgiving because God has been good to me, better than I deserve. He has opened doors for me that I did not know were closed. He opened doors for me in places where I never knew doors existed. Yes, **and still, I cry** - but I cry *Glory,* and I cry *Amen!*